A VIEW FROM THE BRIDGE

ARTHUR MILLER

Notes and activities: Su Fielder

OXFORD

OXFORD
UNIVERSITY PRESS

Great Clarendon Street, Oxford, OX2 6DP, United Kingdom

Oxford University Press is a department of the University of Oxford. It furthers the University's objective of excellence in research, scholarship, and education by publishing worldwide. Oxford is a registered trade mark of Oxford University Press in the UK and in certain other countries

This edition first published in 2019.

British Library Cataloguing in Publication Data

Data available

ISBN 978-019-843836-6

10 9 8 7 6 5 4 3 2

Printed and bound by CPI Group (UK) Ltd, Croydon, CR0 4YY

Acknowledgements

The publisher would like to thank the Arthur Miller Trust for their support in the development of the notes and activities that accompany the text.

The author and publisher are grateful for permission to reprint the following copyright images:

Cover: ClassicStock/Alamy Stock Photo, Robyn Mackenzie/ Shutterstock. **p86**: Central Press/Hulton Archive/Getty Images.

The author and publisher are grateful for permission to include extracts from the following copyright material:

Arthur Miller: *Timebends: A Life* (Bloomsbury, 2012), copyright © Arthur Miller 1987, 1995, reprinted by permission of The Wylie Agency (UK) Ltd.

Arthur Miller: 'Tragedy and the Common Man', first published in the *New York Times*, February 1949, from *The Theatre Essays of Arthur Miller* edited by Robert A Martin (Methuen,1994), copyright © Arthur Miller 1949, 1978, 1994, reprinted by permission of Methuen Drama, an imprint of Bloomsbury Publishing Plc.

We have tried to trace and contact all copyright holders before publication. If notified, the publishers will be pleased to rectify any errors or omissions at the earliest opportunity.

Contents

INTRODUCTION

Key terms

prose
the language of straightforward communication, written without rhythm or rhyme

verse
a style of writing that typically has a rhythm and sometimes rhyme

Arthur Miller was already considered to be one of the foremost American playwrights when his one-act version of *A View from the Bridge* was staged in 1955 at the Coronet Theatre on Broadway. This version was written in **verse**.

The play formed one half of a double bill with *A Memory of Two Mondays*, a semi-autobiographical play based on Miller's experiences as a warehouse worker in Brooklyn during the Depression of the 1930s. Neither play was well-received, and they both had a relatively short run.

Miller added new material and created a two-act, **prose** version of *A View from the Bridge*, giving more prominence to the female characters. This version of the play, the one we now know, was premiered at the Comedy Theatre in London in 1956, directed by Peter Brook, to great critical acclaim. The Comedy Theatre established the New Watergate Theatre Club, also in 1956, which was a private members club. *A View from the Bridge* had been banned by Lord Chamberlain's office for its references to homosexuality; however, the New Watergate Theatre Club allowed the performance of the play (and other unlicensed plays) because they were performed in private to members only. *A View from the Bridge* has become one of Miller's most enduring and frequently produced dramas.

The tragedy of Eddie Carbone, an 'everyman' figure whom Miller cast as the tragic hero of the play, had its beginnings in a story Miller heard as he was researching the lives of the longshoremen (dockers) working in the Red Hook district of Brooklyn. The plot was based on a story that Miller heard about 'a longshoreman who ratted to the Immigration Bureau on two brothers, his own relatives, who were living illegally in his very home, in order to break up an engagement between one of them and his niece' (page 152, *Timebends*).

Later, on a visit to post-war Europe, Miller visited the Italian island of Sicily, where many of the immigrant longshoremen in Brooklyn originally came from, seeing for himself the poverty and hopelessness that existed there, with unemployment at an all-time high. This experience helped to crystalize the plot line for *A View from the Bridge*.

Miller adopted the classical Greek tragedy convention of the chorus, represented by the lawyer Alfieri, who acts as both narrator and moral guide as well as being a character within the plot, helping Miller to tell the story of the downfall of Eddie Carbone in a tautly compressed dramatic style.

Character list

A View from the Bridge was first presented at the New Watergate Theatre Club in London on 11 October 1956, with the following cast:

Louis	**Richard Harris**
Mike	**Norman Mitchell**
Alfieri	**Michael Gwynn**
Eddie	**Anthony Quayle**
Catherine	**Mary Ure**
Beatrice	**Megs Jenkins**
Marco	**Ian Bannen**
Tony	**Ralph Nossek**
Rodolpho	**Brian Bedford**
First Immigration Officer	**John Stone**
Second Immigration Officer	**Colin Rix**
Mr. Lipari	**Mervyn Blake**
Mrs. Lipari	**Catherine Willmer**
A 'Submarine'	**Peter James**

The production was directed and designed by Peter Brook.

The action takes place in and around a tenement house in Brooklyn.

ACT ONE

*The street and house front of a tenement building. The front is skeletal entirely. The main acting area is the living room–dining room of **Eddie's** apartment. It is a worker's flat, clean, sparse, homely. There is a rocker down front; a round dining table at center, with chairs; and a portable phonograph.*

At back are a bedroom door and an opening to the kitchen; none of these interiors are seen.

*At the right, forestage, a desk. This is **Mr. Alfieri's** law office.*

There is also a telephone booth. This is not used until the last scenes, so it may be covered or left in view.

A stairway leads up to the apartment, and then farther up to the next story, which is not seen.

Ramps, representing the street, run upstage and off to right and left.

*As the curtain rises, **Louis** and **Mike**, longshoremen, are pitching coins against the building at left.*

A distant foghorn blows.

*Enter **Alfieri**, a lawyer in his fifties turning gray; he is portly, good-humored, and thoughtful. The two pitchers nod to him as he passes. He crosses the stage to his desk, removes his hat, runs his fingers through his hair, and grinning, speaks to the audience.*

Alfieri   You wouldn't have known it, but something amusing has just happened. You see how uneasily they nod to me? That's because I am a lawyer. In this neighborhood to meet a lawyer or a priest on the street is unlucky. We're only thought of in connection with disasters, and they'd rather not get too close.

I often think that behind that suspicious little nod of theirs lie three thousand years of distrust. A lawyer means the law, and in Sicily, from where their fathers came, the law has not been a friendly idea since the Greeks were beaten.

I am inclined to notice the ruins in things, perhaps because I was born in Italy… I only came here when I was twenty-five. In those days, Al Capone, the greatest Carthaginian of all, was learning his trade on these pavements, and Frankie Yale himself was cut precisely in half by a machine gun on the corner of Union Street, two blocks away. Oh, there were many here who were justly shot by unjust men. Justice is very important here.

But this is Red Hook, not Sicily. This is the slum that faces the bay on the seaward side of Brooklyn Bridge. This is the gullet of New York swallowing the tonnage of the world. And now we are quite civilized, quite American. Now we settle for half, and I like it better. I no longer keep a pistol in my filing cabinet.

And my practice is entirely unromantic.

My wife has warned me, so have my friends; they tell me the people in this neighborhood lack elegance, glamour. After all, who have I dealt with in my life? Longshoremen and their wives, and fathers and grandfathers, compensation cases, evictions, family squabbles – the petty troubles of the poor – and yet… every few years there is still a case, and as the parties tell me what the trouble is, the flat air in my office suddenly washes in with the green scent of the sea, the dust in this air is blown away and the thought comes that in some Caesar's year, in Calabria perhaps or on the cliff at Syracuse, another lawyer, quite differently dressed, heard the same complaint and sat there as powerless as I, and watched it run its bloody course.

Eddie *has appeared and has been pitching coins with the men and is highlighted among them. He is forty – a husky, slightly overweight longshoreman.*

This one's name was Eddie Carbone, a longshoreman working the docks from Brooklyn Bridge to the breakwater where the open sea begins.

Alfieri *walks into darkness.*

Eddie   *[Moving up steps into doorway]* Well, I'll see ya, fellas.

Catherine *enters from kitchen, crosses down to window, looks out.*

Louis   You workin' tomorrow?

Eddie	Yeah, there's another day yet on that ship. See ya, Louis.
	Eddie *goes into the house, as light rises in the apartment.*
	Catherine *is waving to Louis from the window and turns to him.*
Catherine	Hi, Eddie!
	Eddie *is pleased and therefore shy about it; he hangs up his cap and jacket.*
Eddie	Where you goin' all dressed up?
Catherine	*[Running her hands over her skirt]* I just got it. You like it?
Eddie	Yeah, it's nice. And what happened to your hair?
Catherine	You like it? I fixed it different. *[Calling to kitchen]* He's here, B.!
Eddie	Beautiful. Turn around, lemme see in the back. *[She turns for him.]* Oh, if your mother was alive to see you now! She wouldn't believe it.
Catherine	You like it, huh?
Eddie	You look like one of them girls that went to college. Where you goin'?
Catherine	*[Taking his arm]* Wait'll B. comes in, I'll tell you something. Here, sit down. *[She is walking him to the armchair. Calling offstage]* Hurry up, will you, B.?
Eddie	*[Sitting]* What's goin' on?
Catherine	I'll get you a beer, all right?
Eddie	Well, tell me what happened. Come over here, talk to me.
Catherine	I want to wait till B. comes in. *[She sits on her heels beside him.]* Guess how much we paid for the skirt.
Eddie	I think it's too short, ain't it?
Catherine	*[Standing]* No! Not when I stand up.

Eddie   Yeah, but you gotta sit down sometimes.

Catherine   Eddie, it's the style now. *[She walks to show him.]* I mean, if you see me walkin' down the street –

Eddie   Listen, you been givin' me the willies the way you walk down the street, I mean it.

Catherine   Why?

Eddie   Catherine, I don't want to be a pest, but I'm tellin' you you're walkin' wavy.

Catherine   I'm walkin' wavy?

Eddie   Now don't aggravate me, Katie, you are walkin' wavy! I don't like the looks they're givin' you in the candy store. And with them new high heels on the sidewalk – clack, clack, clack. The heads are turnin' like windmills.

Catherine   But those guys look at all the girls, you know that.

Eddie   You ain't 'all the girls.'

Catherine   *[Almost in tears because he disapproves]* What do you want me to do? You want me to –

Eddie   Now don't get mad, kid.

Catherine   Well, I don't know what you want from me.

Eddie   Katie, I promised your mother on her deathbed. I'm responsible for you. You're a baby, you don't understand these things. I mean like when you stand here by the window, wavin' outside.

Catherine   I was wavin' to Louis!

Eddie   Listen, I could tell you things about Louis which you wouldn't wave to him no more.

Catherine	*[Trying to joke him out of his warning]* Eddie, I wish there was one guy you couldn't tell me things about!
Eddie	Catherine, do me a favor, will you? You're gettin' to be a big girl now, you gotta keep yourself more, you can't be so friendly, kid. *[Calls]* Hey, B., what're you doin' in there? *[To Catherine]* Get her in here, will you? I got news for her.
Catherine	*[Starting out]* What?
Eddie	Her cousins landed.
Catherine	*[Clapping her hands together]* No! *[She turns instantly and starts for the kitchen.]* B.! Your cousins!

Beatrice *enters, wiping her hands with a towel.*

Beatrice	*[In the face of Catherine's shout]* What?
Catherine	Your cousins got in!
Beatrice	*[Astounded, turns to Eddie]* What are you talkin' about? Where?
Eddie	I was just knockin' off work before and Tony Bereli come over to me; he says the ship is in the North River.
Beatrice	*[Her hands are clasped at her breast; she seems half in fear, half in unutterable joy.]* They're all right?
Eddie	He didn't see them yet, they're still on board. But as soon as they get off he'll meet them. He figures about ten o'clock they'll be here.
Beatrice	*[Sits, almost weak from tension]* And they'll let them off the ship all right? That's fixed, heh?
Eddie	Sure, they give them regular seamen papers and they walk off with the crew. Don't worry about it, B., there's nothin' to it. Couple of hours they'll be here.
Beatrice	What happened? They wasn't supposed to be till next Thursday.

Eddie	I don't know; they put them on any ship they can get them out on. Maybe the other ship they was supposed to take there was some danger – What you cryin' about?
Beatrice	*[Astounded and afraid]* I'm – I just – I can't believe it! I didn't even buy a new tablecloth; I was gonna wash the walls –
Eddie	Listen, they'll think it's a millionaire's house compared to the way they live. Don't worry about the walls. They'll be thankful. *[To* **Catherine***]* Whyn't you run down buy a tablecloth. Go ahead, here. *[He is reaching into his pocket.]*
Catherine	There's no stores open now.
Eddie	*[To* **Beatrice***]* You was gonna put a new cover on the chair.
Beatrice	I know – well, I thought it was gonna be next week! I was gonna clean the walls, I was gonna wax the floors. *[She stands disturbed.]*
Catherine	*[Pointing upward]* Maybe Mrs. Dondero upstairs –
Beatrice	*[Of the tablecloth]* No, hers is worse than this one. *[Suddenly]* My God, I don't even have nothin' to eat for them! *[She starts for the kitchen.]*
Eddie	*[Reaching out and grabbing her arm]* Hey, hey! Take it easy.
Beatrice	No, I'm just nervous, that's all. *[To* **Catherine***]* I'll make the fish.
Eddie	You're savin' their lives, what're you worryin' about the tablecloth? They probably didn't see a tablecloth in their whole life where they come from.
Beatrice	*[Looking into his eyes]* I'm just worried about you, that's all. I'm worried.
Eddie	Listen, as long as they know where they're gonna sleep.
Beatrice	I told them in the letters. They're sleepin' on the floor.
Eddie	Beatrice, all I'm worried about is you got such a heart that I'll end up on the floor with you, and they'll be in our bed.

Beatrice	All right, stop it.
Eddie	Because as soon as you see a tired relative, I end up on the floor.
Beatrice	When did you end up on the floor?
Eddie	When your father's house burned down I didn't end up on the floor?
Beatrice	Well, their house burned down!
Eddie	Yeah, but it didn't keep burnin' for two weeks!
Beatrice	All right, look, I'll tell them to go someplace else.

She starts into the kitchen.

Eddie	Now wait a minute. Beatrice! *[She halts. He goes to her.]* I just don't want you bein' pushed around, that's all. You got too big a heart. *[He touches her hand.]* What're you so touchy?
Beatrice	I'm just afraid if it don't turn out good you'll be mad at me.
Eddie	Listen, if everybody keeps his mouth shut, nothin' can happen. They'll pay for their board.
Beatrice	Oh, I told them.
Eddie	Then what the hell. *[Pause. He moves.]* It's an honor, B. I mean it. I was just thinkin' before, comin' home, suppose my father didn't come to this country, and I was starvin' like them over there… and I had people in America could keep me a couple of months? The man would be honored to lend me a place to sleep.
Beatrice	*[There are tears in her eyes. She turns to **Catherine**.]* You see what he is? *[She turns and grabs **Eddie's** face in her hands.]* Mmm! You're an angel! God'll bless you. *[He is gratefully smiling.]* You'll see, you'll get a blessing for this!
Eddie	*[Laughing]* I'll settle for my own bed.
Beatrice	Go, Baby, set the table.

Catherine	We didn't tell him about me yet.
Beatrice	Let him eat first, then we'll tell him. Bring everything in. *[She hurries* **Catherine** *out.]*
Eddie	*[Sitting at the table]* What's all that about? Where's she goin'?
Beatrice	Noplace. It's very good news, Eddie. I want you to be happy.
Eddie	What's goin' on?
	Catherine *enters with plates, forks.*
Beatrice	She's got a job.
	Pause. **Eddie** *looks at* **Catherine**, *then back to* **Beatrice**.
Eddie	What job? She's gonna finish school.
Catherine	Eddie, you won't believe it –
Eddie	No – no, you gonna finish school. What kinda job, what do you mean? All of a sudden you –
Catherine	Listen a minute, it's wonderful.
Eddie	It's not wonderful. You'll never get nowheres unless you finish school. You can't take no job. Why didn't you ask me before you take a job?
Beatrice	She's askin' you now, she didn't take nothin' yet.
Catherine	Listen a minute! I came to school this morning and the principal called me out of the class, see? To go to his office.
Eddie	Yeah?
Catherine	So I went in and he says to me he's got my records, y'know? And there's a company wants a girl right away. It ain't exactly a secretary, it's a stenographer first, but pretty soon you get to be secretary. And he says to me that I'm the best student in the whole class –
Beatrice	You hear that?

Eddie   Well why not? Sure she's the best.

Catherine I'm the best student, he says, and if I want, I should take the job and the end of the year he'll let me take the examination and he'll give me the certificate. So I'll save practically a year!

Eddie   *[Strangely nervous]* Where's the job? What company?

Catherine It's a big plumbing company over Nostrand Avenue.

Eddie   Nostrand Avenue and where?

Catherine It's someplace by the Navy Yard.

Beatrice   Fifty dollars a week, Eddie.

Eddie   *[To Catherine, surprised]* Fifty?

Catherine I swear.

               Pause.

Eddie   What about all the stuff you wouldn't learn this year, though?

Catherine There's nothin' more to learn, Eddie, I just gotta practice from now on. I know all the symbols and I know the keyboard. I'll just get faster, that's all. And when I'm workin' I'll keep gettin' better and better, you see?

Beatrice   Work is the best practice anyway.

Eddie   That ain't what I wanted, though.

Catherine Why! It's a great big company –

Eddie   I don't like that neighborhood over there.

Catherine It's a block and a half from the subway, he says.

Eddie   Near the Navy Yard plenty can happen in a block and a half. And a plumbin' company! That's one step over the waterfront. They're practically longshoremen.

Beatrice	Yeah, but she'll be in the office, Eddie.
Eddie	I know she'll be in the office, but that ain't what I had in mind.
Beatrice	Listen, she's gotta go to work sometime.
Eddie	Listen, B., she'll be with a lotta plumbers? And sailors up and down the street? So what did she go to school for?
Catherine	But it's fifty a week, Eddie.
Eddie	Look, did I ask you for money? I supported you this long I support you a little more. Please, do me a favor, will ya? I want you to be with different kind of people. I want you to be in a nice office. Maybe a lawyer's office someplace in New York in one of them nice buildings. I mean if you're gonna get outa here then get out; don't go practically in the same kind of neighborhood.

Pause. **Catherine** *lowers her eyes.*

Beatrice	Go, Baby, bring in the supper. *[***Catherine** *goes out.]* Think about it a little bit, Eddie. Please. She's crazy to start work. It's not a little shop, it's a big company. Some day she could be a secretary. They picked her out of the whole class. *[He is silent, staring down at the tablecloth, fingering the pattern.]* What are you worried about? She could take care of herself. She'll get out of the subway and be in the office in two minutes.
Eddie	*[Somehow sickened]* I know that neighborhood, B., I don't like it.
Beatrice	Listen, if nothin' happened to her in this neighborhood it ain't gonna happen noplace else. *[She turns his face to her.]* Look, you gotta get used to it, she's no baby no more. Tell her to take it. *[He turns his head away.]* You hear me? *[She is angering.]* I don't understand you; she's seventeen years old, you gonna keep her in the house all her life?
Eddie	*[Insulted]* What kinda remark is that?
Beatrice	*[With sympathy but insistent force]* Well, I don't understand when it ends. First it was gonna be when she graduated high school, so she graduated high school. Then it was gonna be when she learned

stenographer, so she learned stenographer. So what're we gonna wait for now? I mean it, Eddie, sometimes I don't understand you; they picked her out of the whole class, it's an honor for her.

Catherine enters with food, which she silently sets on the table. After a moment of watching her face, Eddie breaks into a smile, but it almost seems that tears will form in his eyes.

Eddie	With your hair that way you look like a madonna, you know that? You're the madonna type. *[She doesn't look at him, but continues ladling out food onto the plates.]* You wanna go to work, heh, Madonna?
Catherine	*[Softly]* Yeah.
Eddie	*[With a sense of her childhood, her babyhood, and the years]* All right, go to work. *[She looks at him, then rushes and hugs him.]* Hey, hey! Take it easy! *[He holds her face away from him to look at her.]* What're you cryin' about? *[He is affected by her, but smiles his emotion away.]*
Catherine	*[Sitting at her place]* I just – *[Bursting out]* I'm gonna buy all new dishes with my first pay! *[They laugh warmly.]* I mean it. I'll fix up the whole house! I'll buy a rug!
Eddie	And then you'll move away.
Catherine	No, Eddie!
Eddie	*[Grinning]* Why not? That's life. And you'll come visit on Sundays, then once a month, then Christmas and New Year's, finally.
Catherine	*[Grasping his arm to reassure him and to erase the accusation]* No, please!
Eddie	*[Smiling but hurt]* I only ask you one thing – don't trust nobody. You got a good aunt but she's got too big a heart, you learned bad from her. Believe me.
Beatrice	Be the way you are, Katie, don't listen to him.
Eddie	*[To Beatrice – strangely and quickly resentful]* You lived in a house all your life, what do you know about it? You never worked in your life.

Beatrice	She likes people. What's wrong with that?
Eddie	Because most people ain't people. She's goin' to work; plumbers; they'll chew her to pieces if she don't watch out. *[To* **Catherine***]* Believe me, Katie, the less you trust, the less you be sorry.

Eddie *crosses himself and the women do the same, and they eat.*

Catherine	First thing I'll buy is a rug, heh, B.?
Beatrice	I don't mind. *[To* **Eddie***]* I smelled coffee all day today. You unloadin' coffee today?
Eddie	Yeah, a Brazil ship.
Catherine	I smelled it too. It smelled all over the neighborhood.
Eddie	That's one time, boy, to be a longshoreman is a pleasure. I could work coffee ships twenty hours a day. You go down in the hold, y'know? It's like flowers, that smell. We'll bust a bag tomorrow, I'll bring you some.
Beatrice	Just be sure there's no spiders in it, will ya? I mean it. *[She directs this to* **Catherine**, *rolling her eyes upward.]* I still remember that spider coming out of that bag he brung home. I nearly died.
Eddie	You call that a spider? You oughta see what comes outa the bananas sometimes.
Beatrice	Don't talk about it!
Eddie	I seen spiders could stop a Buick.
Beatrice	*[Clapping her hands over her ears]* All right, shut up!
Eddie	*[Laughing and taking a watch out of his pocket]* Well, who started with spiders?
Beatrice	All right, I'm sorry, I didn't mean it. Just don't bring none home again. What time is it?

Eddie	Quarter nine. *[Puts watch back in his pocket. They continue eating in silence.]*
Catherine	He's bringin' them ten o'clock, Tony?
Eddie	Around, yeah. *[He eats.]*
Catherine	Eddie, suppose somebody asks if they're livin' here. *[He looks at her as though already she had divulged something publicly. Defensively]* I mean if they ask.
Eddie	Now look, Baby, I can see we're gettin' mixed up again here.
Catherine	No, I just mean… people'll see them goin' in and out.
Eddie	I don't care who sees them goin' in and out as long as you don't see them goin' in and out. And this goes for you too, B. You don't see nothin' and you don't know nothin'.
Beatrice	What do you mean? I understand.
Eddie	You don't understand; you still think you can talk about this to somebody just a little bit. Now lemme say it once and for all, because you're makin' me nervous again, both of you. I don't care if somebody comes in the house and sees them sleepin' on the floor, it never comes out of your mouth who they are or what they're doin' here.
Beatrice	Yeah, but my mother'll know –
Eddie	Sure she'll know, but just don't you be the one who told her, that's all. This is the United States government you're playin' with now, this is the Immigration Bureau. If you said it you knew it, if you didn't say it you didn't know it.
Catherine	Yeah, but Eddie, suppose somebody –
Eddie	I don't care what question it is. You – don't – know – nothin'. They got stool pigeons all over this neighborhood they're payin' them every week for information, and you don't know who they are. It could be your best friend. You hear? *[To **Beatrice**]* Like Vinny Bolzano, remember Vinny?

Beatrice	Oh, yeah. God forbid.
Eddie	Tell her about Vinny. *[To* **Catherine***]* You think I'm blowin' steam here? *[To* **Beatrice***]* Go ahead, tell her. *[To* **Catherine***]* You was a baby then. There was a family lived next door to her mother, he was about sixteen –
Beatrice	No, he was no more than fourteen, cause I was to his confirmation in Saint Agnes. But the family had an uncle that they were hidin' in the house, and he snitched to the Immigration.
Catherine	The kid snitched?
Eddie	On his own uncle!
Catherine	What, was he crazy?
Eddie	He was crazy after, I tell you that, boy.
Beatrice	Oh, it was terrible. He had five brothers and the old father. And they grabbed him in the kitchen and pulled him down the stairs – three flights his head was bouncin' like a coconut. And they spit on him in the street, his own father and his brothers. The whole neighborhood was cryin'.
Catherine	Ts! So what happened to him?
Beatrice	I think he went away. *[To* **Eddie***]* I never seen him again, did you?
Eddie	*[Rises during this, taking out his watch]* Him? You'll never see him no more, a guy do a thing like that? How's he gonna show his face? *[To* **Catherine,** *as he gets up uneasily]* Just remember, kid, you can quicker get back a million dollars that was stole than a word that you gave away. *[He is standing now, stretching his back.]*
Catherine	Okay, I won't say a word to nobody, I swear.
Eddie	Gonna rain tomorrow. We'll be slidin' all over the decks. Maybe you oughta put something on for them, they be here soon.
Beatrice	I only got fish, I hate to spoil it if they ate already. I'll wait, it only takes a few minutes; I could broil it.

Catherine	What happens, Eddie, when that ship pulls out and they ain't on it, though? Don't the captain say nothin'?
Eddie	*[Slicing an apple with his pocket knife]* Captain's pieced off, what do you mean?
Catherine	Even the captain?
Eddie	What's the matter, the captain don't have to live? Captain gets a piece, maybe one of the mates, piece for the guy in Italy who fixed the papers for them, Tony here'll get a little bite...
Beatrice	I just hope they get work here, that's all I hope.
Eddie	Oh, the syndicate'll fix jobs for them; till they pay 'em off they'll get them work every day. It's after the pay-off, then they'll have to scramble like the rest of us.
Beatrice	Well, it be better than they got there.
Eddie	Oh sure, well, listen. So you gonna start Monday, heh, Madonna?
Catherine	*[Embarrassed]* I'm supposed to, yeah.
	Eddie *is standing facing the two seated women. First* **Beatrice** *smiles, then* **Catherine**, *for a powerful emotion is on him, a childish one and a knowing fear, and the tears show in his eyes – and they are shy before the avowal.*
Eddie	*[Sadly smiling, yet somehow proud of her]* Well... I hope you have good luck. I wish you the best. You know that, kid.
Catherine	*[Rising, trying to laugh]* You sound like I'm goin' a million miles!
Eddie	I know. I guess I just never figured on one thing.
Catherine	*[Smiling]* What?
Eddie	That you would ever grow up. *[He utters a soundless laugh at himself, feeling his breast pocket of his shirt.]* I left a cigar in my other coat, I think. *[He starts for the bedroom.]*

Catherine	Stay there! I'll get it for you.

*She hurries out. There is a slight pause, and **Eddie** turns to **Beatrice**, who has been avoiding his gaze.*

Eddie	What are you mad at me lately?
Beatrice	Who's mad? [She gets up, clearing the dishes.] I'm not mad. [She picks up the dishes and turns to him.] You're the one is mad. [She turns and goes into the kitchen as **Catherine** enters from the bedroom with a cigar and a pack of matches.]
Catherine	Here! I'll light it for you! [She strikes a match and holds it to his cigar. He puffs. Quietly] Don't worry about me, Eddie, heh?
Eddie	Don't burn yourself. [Just in time she blows out the match.] You better go in help her with the dishes.
Catherine	[Turns quickly to the table, and, seeing the table cleared, she says, almost guiltily] Oh! [She hurries into the kitchen, and as she exits there] I'll do the dishes, B.!

*Alone, **Eddie** stands looking toward the kitchen for a moment. Then he takes out his watch, glances at it, replaces it in his pocket, sits in the armchair, and stares at the smoke flowing out of his mouth.*

*The lights go down, then come up on **Alfieri**, who has moved onto the forestage.*

Alfieri	He was as good a man as he had to be in a life that was hard and even. He worked on the piers when there was work, he brought home his pay, and he lived. And toward ten o'clock of that night, after they had eaten, the cousins came.

*The lights fade on **Alfieri** and rise on the street.*

*Enter **Tony**, escorting **Marco** and **Rodolpho**, each with a valise. **Tony** halts, indicates the house. They stand for a moment looking at it.*

Marco	[He is a square-built peasant of thirty-two, suspicious, tender, and quiet-voiced.] Thank you.
Tony	You're on your own now. Just be careful, that's all. Ground floor.
Marco	Thank you.
Tony	[Indicating the house] I'll see you on the pier tomorrow. You'll go to work.

Marco nods. Tony continues on walking down the street.

Rodolpho	This will be the first house I ever walked into in America! Imagine! She said they were poor!
Marco	Ssh! Come. They go to door.

Marco knocks. The lights rise in the room. Eddie goes and opens the door. Enter Marco and Rodolpho, removing their caps. Beatrice and Catherine enter from the kitchen. The lights fade in the street.

Eddie	You Marco?
Marco	Marco.
Eddie	Come on in! [He shakes Marco's hand.]
Beatrice	Here, take the bags!
Marco	[Nods, looks to the women and fixes on Beatrice. Crosses to Beatrice] Are you my cousin?

She nods. He kisses her hand.

Beatrice	[Above the table, touching her chest with her hand] Beatrice. This is my husband, Eddie. [All nod.] Catherine, my sister Nancy's daughter. [The brothers nod.]
Marco	[Indicating Rodolpho] My brother. Rodolpho. [Rodolpho nods. Marco comes with a certain formal stiffness to Eddie.] I want to tell you now Eddie – when you say go, we will go.

23

Eddie	Oh, no… *[Takes **Marco's** bag]*
Marco	I see it's a small house, but soon, maybe, we can have our own house.
Eddie	You're welcome, Marco, we got plenty of room here. Katie, give them supper, heh? *[Exits into bedroom with their bags]*
Catherine	Come here, sit down. I'll get you some soup.
Marco	*[As they go to the table]* We ate on the ship. Thank you. *[To **Eddie**, calling off to bedroom]* Thank you.
Beatrice	Get some coffee. We'll all have coffee. Come sit down.

Rodolpho and **Marco** *sit at the table.*

Catherine	*[Wondrously]* How come he's so dark and you're so light, Rodolpho?
Rodolpho	*[Ready to laugh]* I don't know. A thousand years ago, they say, the Danes invaded Sicily.

Beatrice *kisses* **Rodolpho**. *They laugh as* **Eddie** *enters.*

Catherine	*[To **Beatrice**]* He's practically blond!
Eddie	How's the coffee doin'?
Catherine	*[Brought up]* I'm gettin' it. *[She hurries out to kitchen.]*
Eddie	*[Sits on his rocker]* Yiz have a nice trip?
Marco	The ocean is always rough. But we are good sailors.
Eddie	No trouble gettin' here?
Marco	No. The man brought us. Very nice man.
Rodolpho	*[To **Eddie**]* He says we start to work tomorrow. Is he honest?
Eddie	*[Laughing]* No. But as long as you owe them money, they'll get you plenty of work. *[To **Marco**]* Yiz ever work on the piers in Italy?

Marco	Piers? Ts! – no.
Rodolpho	*[Smiling at the smallness of his town]* In our town there are no piers, only the beach, and little fishing boats.
Beatrice	So what kinda work did yiz do?
Marco	*[Shrugging shyly, even embarrassed]* Whatever there is, anything.
Rodolpho	Sometimes they build a house, or if they fix the bridge – Marco is a mason and I bring him the cement. *[He laughs.]* In harvest time we work in the fields… if there is work. Anything.
Eddie	Still bad there, heh?
Marco	Bad, yes.
Rodolpho	*[laughing]* It's terrible! We stand around all day in the piazza listening to the fountain like birds. Everybody waits only for the train.
Beatrice	What's on the train?
Rodolpho	Nothing. But if there are many passengers and you're lucky you make a few lire to push the taxi up the hill.
	Enter **Catherine**. *She listens.*
Beatrice	You gotta push a taxi?
Rodolpho	*[Laughing]* Oh, sure! It's a feature in our town. The horses in our town are skinnier than goats. So if there are too many passengers we help to push the carriages up to the hotel. *[He laughs.]* In our town the horses are only for show.
Catherine	Why don't they have automobile taxis?
Rodolpho	There is one. We push that too. *[They laugh.]* Everything in our town, you gotta push!
Beatrice	*[To* **Eddie***]* How do you like that!

Eddie	*[To Marco]* So what're you wanna do, you gonna stay here in this country or you wanna go back?
Marco	*[Surprised]* Go back?
Eddie	Well, you're married, ain't you?
Marco	Yes. I have three children.
Beatrice	Three! I thought only one.
Marco	Oh, no. I have three now. Four years, five years, six years.
Beatrice	Ah… I bet they're cryin' for you already, heh?
Marco	What can I do? The older one is sick in his chest. My wife – she feeds them from her own mouth. I tell you the truth, if I stay there they will never grow up. They eat the sunshine.
Beatrice	My God. So how long you want to stay?
Marco	With your permission, we will stay maybe a –
Eddie	She don't mean in this house, she means in the country.
Marco	Oh. Maybe four, five, six years, I think.
Rodolpho	*[Smiling]* He trusts his wife.
Beatrice	Yeah, but maybe you'll get enough, you'll be able to go back quicker.
Marco	I hope. I don't know. *[To **Eddie**]* I understand it's not so good here either.
Eddie	Oh, you guys'll be all right – till you pay them off, anyway. After that, you'll have to scramble, that's all. But you'll make better here than you could there.
Rodolpho	How much? We hear all kinds of figures. How much can a man make? We work hard, we'll work all day, all night –

Marco *raises a hand to hush him.*

Eddie	*[He is coming more and more to address **Marco** only.]* On the average a whole year? Maybe – well, it's hard to say, see. Sometimes we lay off, there's no ships three four weeks.
Marco	Three, four weeks! – Ts!
Eddie	But I think you could probably – thirty, forty a week, over the whole twelve months of the year.
Marco	*[Rises, crosses to **Eddie**]* Dollars.
Eddie	Sure dollars.

Marco *puts an arm round **Rodolpho** and they laugh.*

Marco	If we can stay here a few months, Beatrice –
Beatrice	Listen, you're welcome, Marco –
Marco	Because I could send them a little more if I stay here.
Beatrice	As long as you want, we got plenty a room.
Marco	*[His eyes are showing tears.]* My wife – *[To **Eddie**]* My wife – I want to send right away maybe twenty dollars –
Eddie	You could send them something next week already.
Marco	*[He is near tears.]* Eduardo… *[He goes to **Eddie**, offering his hand.]*
Eddie	Don't thank me. Listen, what the hell, it's no skin off me. *[To **Catherine**]* What happened to the coffee?
Catherine	I got it on. *[To **Rodolpho**]* You married too? No.
Rodolpho	*[Rises]* Oh, no…
Beatrice	*[To **Catherine**]* I told you he –
Catherine	I know, I just thought maybe he got married recently.

Rodolpho	I have no money to get married. I have a nice face, but no money. *[He laughs.]*
Catherine	*[To **Beatrice**]* He's a real blond!
Beatrice	*[To **Rodolpho**]* You want to stay here too, heh? For good?
Rodolpho	Me? Yes, forever! Me, I want to be an American. And then I want to go back to Italy when I am rich, and I will buy a motorcycle. *[He smiles.* **Marco** *shakes him affectionately.]*
Catherine	A motorcycle!
Rodolpho	With a motorcycle in Italy you will never starve any more.
Beatrice	I'll get you coffee. *[She exits to the kitchen.]*
Eddie	What you do with a motorcycle?
Marco	He dreams, he dreams.
Rodolpho	*[To **Marco**]* Why? *[To **Eddie**]* Messages! The rich people in the hotel always need someone who will carry a message. But quickly, and with a great noise. With a blue motorcycle I would station myself in the courtyard of the hotel, and in a little while I would have messages.
Marco	When you have no wife you have dreams.
Eddie	Why can't you just walk, or take a trolley or sump'm?
	*Enter **Beatrice** with coffee.*
Rodolpho	Oh, no, the machine, the machine is necessary. A man comes into a great hotel and says, I am a messenger. Who is this man? He disappears walking, there is no noise, nothing. Maybe he will never come back, maybe he will never deliver the message. But a man who rides up on a great machine, this man is responsible, this man exists. He will be given messages. *[He helps **Beatrice** set out the coffee things.]* I am also a singer, though.
Eddie	You mean a regular – ?

Rodolpho	Oh, yes. One night last year Andreola got sick. Baritone. And I took his place in the garden of the hotel. Three arias I sang without a mistake! Thousand-lire notes they threw from the tables, money was falling like a storm in the treasury. It was magnificent. We lived six months on that night, eh, Marco?

Marco *nods doubtfully.*

Marco	Two months.

Eddie *laughs.*

Beatrice	Can't you get a job in that place?
Rodolpho	Andreola got better. He's a baritone, very strong.

Beatrice *laughs.*

Marco	*[Regretfully, to Beatrice]* He sang too loud.
Rodolpho	Why too loud?
Marco	Too loud. The guests in that hotel are all Englishmen. They don't like too loud.
Rodolpho	*[To Catherine]* Nobody ever said it was too loud!
Marco	I say. It was too loud. *[To Beatrice]* I knew it as soon as he started to sing. Too loud.
Rodolpho	Then why did they throw so much money?
Marco	They paid for your courage. The English like courage. But once is enough.
Rodolpho	*[To all but Marco]* I never heard anybody say it was too loud.
Catherine	Did you ever hear of jazz?
Rodolpho	Oh, sure! I sing jazz.
Catherine	*[Rises]* You could sing jazz?

Rodolpho	Oh, I sing Napolidan, jazz, bel canto – I sing 'Paper Doll', you like 'Paper Doll'?
Catherine	Oh, sure, I'm crazy for 'Paper Doll'. Go ahead, sing it.

Rodolpho *takes his stance after getting a nod of permission from* **Marco**, *and with a high tenor voice begins singing:*

I'll tell you boys it's tough to be alone,
And it's tough to love a doll that's not your own.
I'm through with all of them,
I'll never fall again,
Hey, boy, what you gonna do?
I'm gonna buy a paper doll that I can call my own,
A doll that other fellows cannot steal.

Eddie *rises and moves upstage.*

And then those flirty, flirty guys
With their flirty, flirty eyes
Will have to flirt with dollies that are real –

Eddie	Hey, kid – hey, wait a minute –
Catherine	*[Enthralled]* Leave him finish, it's beautiful! *[To* **Beatrice***]* He's terrific! It's terrific, Rodolpho.
Eddie	Look, kid; you don't want to be picked up, do ya?
Marco	No – no! *[He rises.]*
Eddie	*[Indicating the rest of the building]* Because we never had no singers here… and all of a sudden there's a singer in the house, y'know what I mean?
Marco	Yes, yes. You'll be quiet, Rodolpho.
Eddie	*[He is flushed.]* They got guys all over the place, Marco. I mean.
Marco	Yes. He'll be quiet. *[To* **Rodolpho***]* You'll be quiet.

Rodolpho *nods.*

Eddie *has risen, with iron control, even a smile. He moves to* **Catherine***.*

Eddie   What's the high heels for, Garbo?

Catherine   I figured for tonight –

Eddie   Do me a favor, will you? Go ahead.

Embarrassed now, angered, **Catherine** *goes out into the bedroom.* **Beatrice** *watches her go and gets up; in passing, she gives* **Eddie** *a cold look, restrained only by the strangers, and goes to the table to pour coffee.*

Eddie   *[Striving to laugh, and to* **Marco***, but directed as much to* **Beatrice***]* All actresses they want to be around here.

Rodolpho   *[Happy about it]* In Italy too! All the girls.

Catherine *emerges from the bedroom in low-heel shoes, comes to the table.* **Rodolpho** *is lifting a cup.*

Eddie   *[He is sizing up* **Rodolpho***, and there is a concealed suspicion]* Yeah, heh?

Rodolpho   Yes! *[Laughs, indicating* **Catherine***]* Especially when they are so beautiful!

Catherine   You like sugar?

Rodolpho   Sugar? Yes! I like sugar very much!

Eddie *is downstage, watching as she pours a spoonful of sugar into his cup, his face puffed with trouble, and the room dies.*

Lights rise on **Alfieri***.*

Alfieri   Who can ever know what will be discovered? Eddie Carbone had never expected to have a destiny. A man works, raises his family, goes bowling, eats, gets old, and then he dies. Now, as the weeks passed, there was a future, there was a trouble that would not go away.

*The lights fade on **Alfieri**, then rise on **Eddie** standing at the doorway of the house. **Beatrice** enters on the street. She sees **Eddie**, smiles at him. He looks away.*

*She starts to enter the house when **Eddie** speaks.*

Eddie	It's after eight.
Beatrice	Well, it's a long show at the Paramount.
Eddie	They must've seen every picture in Brooklyn by now. He's supposed to stay in the house when he ain't working. He ain't supposed to go advertising himself.
Beatrice	Well that's his trouble, what do you care? If they pick him up they pick him up, that's all. Come in the house.
Eddie	What happened to the stenography? I don't see her practice no more.
Beatrice	She'll get back to it. She's excited, Eddie.
Eddie	She tell you anything?
Beatrice	*[Comes to him, now the subject is opened]* What's the matter with you? He's a nice kid, what do you want from him?
Eddie	That's a nice kid? He gives me the heeby-jeebies.
Beatrice	*[Smiling]* Ah, go on, you're just jealous.
Eddie	Of *him*? Boy, you don't think much of me.
Beatrice	I don't understand you. What's so terrible about him?
Eddie	You mean it's all right with you? That's gonna be her husband?
Beatrice	Why? He's a nice fella, hard workin', he's a good-lookin' fella.
Eddie	He sings on the ships, didja know that?
Beatrice	What do you mean, he sings?

Eddie	Just what I said, he sings. Right on the deck, all of a sudden, a whole song comes out of his mouth – with motions. You know what they're callin' him now? Paper Doll they're callin' him, Canary. He's like a weird. He comes out on the pier, one-two-three, it's a regular free show.
Beatrice	Well, he's a kid; he don't know how to behave himself yet.
Eddie	And with that wacky hair; he's like a chorus girl or sump'm.
Beatrice	So he's blond, so –
Eddie	I just hope that's his regular hair, that's all I hope.
Beatrice	You crazy or sump'm? *[She tries to turn him to her.]*
Eddie	*[He keeps his head turned away.]* What's so crazy? I don't like his whole way.
Beatrice	Listen, you never seen a blond guy in your life? What about Whitey Balso?
Eddie	*[Turning to her victoriously]* Sure, but Whitey don't sing; he don't do like that on the ships.
Beatrice	Well, maybe that's the way they do in Italy.
Eddie	Then why don't his brother sing? Marco goes around like a man; nobody kids Marco. *[He moves from her, halts. She realizes there is a campaign solidified in him.]* I tell you the truth I'm surprised I have to tell you all this. I mean I'm surprised, B.
Beatrice	*[She goes to him with purpose now.]* Listen, you ain't gonna start nothin' here.
Eddie	I ain't startin' nothin', but I ain't gonna stand around lookin' at that. For that character I didn't bring her up. I swear, B., I'm surprised at you; I sit there waitin' for you to wake up but everything is great with you.
Beatrice	No, everything ain't great with me.
Eddie	No?

Beatrice	No. But I got other worries.
Eddie	Yeah. *[He is already weakening.]*
Beatrice	Yeah, you want me to tell you?
Eddie	*[In retreat]* Why? What worries you got?
Beatrice	When am I gonna be a wife again, Eddie?
Eddie	I ain't been feelin' good. They bother me since they came.
Beatrice	It's almost three months you don't feel good; they're only here a couple of weeks. It's three months, Eddie.
Eddie	I don't know, B. I don't want to talk about it.
Beatrice	What's the matter, Eddie, you don't like me, heh?
Eddie	What do you mean, I don't like you? I said I don't feel good, that's all.
Beatrice	Well, tell me, am I doing something wrong? Talk to me.
Eddie	*[Pause. He can't speak, then]* I can't. I can't talk about it.
Beatrice	Well tell me what –
Eddie	I got nothin' to say about it!

She stands for a moment; he is looking off; she turns to go into the house.

Eddie	I'll be all right, B.; just lay off me, will ya? I'm worried about her.
Beatrice	The girl is gonna be eighteen years old, it's time already.
Eddie	B., he's taking her for a ride!
Beatrice	All right, that's her ride. What're you gonna stand over her till she's forty? Eddie, I want you to cut it out now, you hear me? I don't like it! Now come in the house.
Eddie	I want to take a walk, I'll be in right away.

Beatrice	They ain't goin' to come any quicker if you stand in the street. It ain't nice, Eddie.
Eddie	I'll be in right away. Go ahead. *[He walks off.]*
	She goes into the house. **Eddie** *glances up the street, sees* **Louis** *and* **Mike** *coming, and sits on an iron railing.* **Louis** *and* **Mike** *enter.*
Louis	Wanna go bowlin' tonight?
Eddie	I'm too tired. Goin' to sleep.
Louis	How's your two submarines?
Eddie	They're okay.
Louis	I see they're gettin' work allatime.
Eddie	Oh yeah, they're doin' all right.
Mike	That's what we oughta do. We oughta leave the country and come in under the water. Then we get work.
Eddie	You ain't kiddin'.
Louis	Well, what the hell. Y'know?
Eddie	Sure.
Louis	*[Sits on railing beside* **Eddie***]* Believe me, Eddie, you got a lotta credit comin' to you.
Eddie	Aah, they don't bother me, don't cost me nutt'n.
Mike	That older one, boy, he's a regular bull. I seen him the other day liftin' coffee bags over the Matson Line. They leave him alone he woulda load the whole ship by himself.
Eddie	Yeah, he's a strong guy, that guy. Their father was a regular giant, supposed to be.
Louis	Yeah, you could see. He's a regular slave.

Mike *[Grinning]* That blond one, though – *[**Eddie** looks at him.]* He's got a sense of humor. *[Louis snickers.]*

Eddie *[Searchingly]* Yeah. He's funny –

Mike *[Starting to laugh]* Well he ain't exackly funny, but he's always like makin' remarks like, y'know? He comes around, everybody's laughin'. *[**Louis** laughs.]*

Eddie *[Uncomfortably, grinning]* Yeah, well… he's got a sense of humor.

Mike *[Laughing]* Yeah, I mean, he's always makin' like remarks, like, y'know?

Eddie Yeah, I know. But he's a kid yet, y'know? He – he's just a kid, that's all.

Mike *[Getting hysterical with **Louis**]* I know. You take one look at him – everybody's happy. *[**Louis** laughs.]* I worked one day with him last week over the Moore–MacCormack Line, I'm tellin' you they was all hysterical. *[**Louis** and he explode in laughter.]*

Eddie Why? What'd he do?

Mike I don't know… he was just humorous. You never can remember what he says, y'know? But it's the way he says it. I mean he gives you a look sometimes and you start laughin'!

Eddie Yeah. *[Troubled]* He's got a sense of humor.

Mike *[Gasping]* Yeah.

Louis *[Rising]* Well, we see ya, Eddie.

Eddie Take it easy.

Louis Yeah. See ya.

Mike If you wanna come bowlin' later we're goin' Flatbush Avenue.

*Laughing, they move to exit, meeting **Rodolpho** and **Catherine** entering on the street. Their laughter rises as they see **Rodolpho**, who does not understand but joins in. **Eddie** moves to enter the house as **Louis** and **Mike** exit. **Catherine** stops him at the door.*

Catherine	Hey, Eddie – what a picture we saw! Did we laugh!
Eddie	*[He can't help smiling at sight of her.]* Where'd you go?
Catherine	Paramount. It was with those two guys, y'know? That –
Eddie	Brooklyn Paramount?
Catherine	*[With an edge of anger, embarrassed before Rodolpho]* Sure, the Brooklyn Paramount. I told you we wasn't goin' to New York.
Eddie	*[Retreating before the threat of her anger]* All right, I only asked you. *[To Rodolpho]* I just don't want her hangin' around Times Square, see? It's full of tramps over there.
Rodolpho	I would like to go to Broadway once, Eddie. I would like to walk with her once where the theaters are and the opera. Since I was a boy I see pictures of those lights.
Eddie	*[His little patience waning]* I want to talk to her a minute, Rodolpho. Go inside, will you?
Rodolpho	Eddie, we only walk together in the streets. She teaches me.
Catherine	You know what he can't get over? That there's no fountains in Brooklyn!
Eddie	*[Smiling unwillingly]* Fountains? **[Rodolpho smiles at his own naïveté.]**
Catherine	In Italy he says, every town's got fountains, and they meet there. And you know what? They got oranges on the trees where he comes from, and lemons. Imagine – on the trees? I mean it's interesting. But he's crazy for New York.
Rodolpho	*[Attempting familiarity]* Eddie, why can't we go once to Broadway – ?
Eddie	Look, I gotta tell her something –
Rodolpho	Maybe you can come too. I want to see all those lights. *[He sees no response in Eddie's face. He glances at Catherine.]* I'll walk by the river before I go to sleep. *[He walks off down the street.]*

Catherine	Why don't you talk to him, Eddie? He blesses you, and you don't talk to him hardly.
Eddie	*[Enveloping her with his eyes]* I bless you and you don't talk to me. *[He tries to smile.]*
Catherine	I don't talk to you? *[She hits his arm.]* What do you mean?
Eddie	I don't see you no more. I come home you're runnin' around someplace –
Catherine	Well, he wants to see everything, that's all, so we go... You mad at me?
Eddie	No. *[He moves from her, smiling sadly.]* It's just I used to come home, you was always there. Now, I turn around, you're a big girl. I don't know how to talk to you.
Catherine	Why?
Eddie	I don't know, you're runnin', you're runnin', Katie. I don't think you listening any more to me.
Catherine	*[Going to him]* Ah, Eddie, sure I am. What's the matter? You don't like him?
	Slight pause.
Eddie	*[Turns to her]* You like him, Katie?
Catherine	*[With a blush but holding her ground]* Yeah. I like him.
Eddie	*[His smile goes]* You like him.
Catherine	*[Looking down]* Yeah. *[Now she looks at him for the consequences, smiling but tense. He looks at her like a lost boy.]* What're you got against him? I don't understand. He only blesses you.
Eddie	*[Turns away]* He don't bless me, Katie.
Catherine	He does! You're like a father to him!
Eddie	*[Turns to her]* Katie.

Catherine	What, Eddie?
Eddie	You gonna marry him?
Catherine	I don't know. We just been… goin' around, that's all. *[Turns to him]* What're you got against him, Eddie? Please, tell me. What?
Eddie	He don't respect you.
Catherine	Why?
Eddie	Katie… if you wasn't an orphan, wouldn't he ask your father's permission before he run around with you like this?
Catherine	Oh, well, he didn't think you'd mind.
Eddie	He knows I mind, but it don't bother him if I mind, don't you see that?
Catherine	No, Eddie, he's got all kinds of respect for me. And you too! We walk across the street he takes my arm – he almost bows to me! You got him all wrong, Eddie; I mean it, you –
Eddie	Katie, he's only bowin' to his passport.
Catherine	His passport!
Eddie	That's right. He marries you he's got the right to be an American citizen. That's what's goin' on here. *[She is puzzled and surprised.]* You understand what I'm tellin' you? The guy is lookin' for his break, that's all he's lookin' for.
Catherine	*[Pained]* Oh, no, Eddie, I don't think so.
Eddie	You don't think so! Katie, you're gonna make me cry here. Is that a workin' man? What does he do with his first money? A snappy new jacket he buys, records, a pointy pair new shoes and his brother's kids are starvin' over there with tuberculosis? That's a hit-and-run guy, Baby; he's got bright lights in his head, Broadway. Them guys don't think of nobody but theirself! You marry him and the next time you see him it'll be for divorce!

Catherine	*[Steps toward him]* Eddie, he never said a word about his papers or –
Eddie	You mean he's supposed to tell you that?
Catherine	I don't think he's even thinking about it.
Eddie	What's better for him to think about! He could be picked up any day here and he's back pushin' taxis up the hill!
Catherine	No, I don't believe it.
Eddie	Katie, don't break my heart, listen to me.
Catherine	I don't want to hear it.
Eddie	Katie, listen…
Catherine	He loves me!
Eddie	*[With deep alarm]* Don't say that, for God's sake! This is the oldest racket in the country –
Catherine	*[Desperately, as though he had made his imprint]* I don't believe it! *[She rushes to the house.]*
Eddie	*[Following her]* They been pullin' this since the Immigration Law was put in! They grab a green kid that don't know nothin' and they –
Catherine	*[Sobbing]* I don't believe it and I wish to hell you'd stop it!
Eddie	Katie!
	They enter the apartment. The lights in the living room have risen and **Beatrice** *is there. She looks past the sobbing* **Catherine** *at* **Eddie**, *who, in the presence of his wife, makes an awkward gesture of eroded command, indicating* **Catherine**.
Eddie	Why don't you straighten her out?
Beatrice	*[Inwardly angered at his flowing emotion, which in itself alarms her]* When are you going to leave her alone?

Eddie	B., the guy is no good!
Beatrice	*[Suddenly, with open fright and fury]* You going to leave her alone? Or you gonna drive me crazy? *[He turns, striving to retain his dignity, but nevertheless in guilt walks out of the house, into the street and away.* **Catherine** *starts into a bedroom.]* Listen, Catherine. *[***Catherine** *halts, turns to her sheepishly.]* What are you going to do with yourself?
Catherine	I don't know.
Beatrice	Don't tell me you don't know; you're not a baby any more, what are you going to do with yourself?
Catherine	He won't listen to me.
Beatrice	I don't understand this. He's not your father, Catherine. I don't understand what's going on here.
Catherine	*[As one who herself is trying to rationalize a buried impulse]* What am I going to do, just kick him in the face with it?
Beatrice	Look, honey, you wanna get married, or don't you wanna get married? What are you worried about, Katie?
Catherine	*[Quietly, trembling]* I don't know B. It just seems wrong if he's against it so much.
Beatrice	*[Never losing her aroused alarm]* Sit down, honey, I want to tell you something. Here, sit down. Was there ever any fella he liked for you? There wasn't, was there?
Catherine	But he says Rodolpho's just after his papers.
Beatrice	Look, he'll say anything. What does he care what he says? If it was a prince came here for you it would be no different. You know that, don't you?
Catherine	Yeah, I guess.
Beatrice	So what does that mean?

Catherine	*[Slowly turns her head to* **Beatrice***]* What?
Beatrice	It means you gotta be your own self more. You still think you're a little girl, honey. But nobody else can make up your mind for you any more, you understand? You gotta give him to understand that he can't give you orders no more.
Catherine	Yeah, but how am I going to do that? He thinks I'm a baby.
Beatrice	Because you think you're a baby. I told you fifty times already, you can't act the way you act. You still walk around in front of him in your slip –
Catherine	Well I forgot.
Beatrice	Well you can't do it. Or like you sit on the edge of the bathtub talkin' to him when he's shavin' in his underwear.
Catherine	When'd I do that?
Beatrice	I seen you in there this morning.
Catherine	Oh… well, I wanted to tell him something and I –
Beatrice	I know, honey. But if you act like a baby and he be treatin' you like a baby. Like when he comes home sometimes you throw yourself at him like when you was twelve years old.
Catherine	Well I like to see him and I'm happy so I –
Beatrice	Look, I'm not tellin' you what to do honey, but –
Catherine	No, you could tell me, B.! Gee, I'm all mixed up. See, I – He looks so sad now and it hurts me.
Beatrice	Well look Katie, if it's goin' to hurt you so much you're gonna end up an old maid here.
Catherine	No!
Beatrice	I'm tellin' you, I'm not makin' a joke. I tried to tell you a couple of times in the last year or so. That's why I was so happy you were going to go

out and get work, you wouldn't be here so much, you'd be a little more independent. I mean it. It's wonderful for a whole family to love each other, but you're a grown woman and you're in the same house with a grown man. So you'll act different now, heh?

Catherine   Yeah, I will. I'll remember.

Beatrice   Because it ain't only up to him, Katie, you understand? I told him the same thing already.

Catherine   *[Quickly]* What?

Beatrice   That he should let you go. But, you see, if only I tell him, he thinks I'm just bawlin' him out, or maybe I'm jealous or somethin', you know?

Catherine   *[Astonished]* He said you was jealous?

Beatrice   No, I'm just sayin' maybe that's what he thinks. *[She reaches over to* **Catherine's** *hand with a strained smile.]* You think I'm jealous of you, honey?

Catherine   No! It's the first I thought of it.

Beatrice   *[With a quiet, sad laugh]* Well you should have thought of it before… but I'm not. We'll be all right. Just give him to understand; you don't have to fight, you're just – You're a woman, that's all, and you got a nice boy, and now the time came when you said good-bye. All right?

Catherine   *[Strangely moved at the prospect]* All right… If I can.

Beatrice   Honey… you gotta.

Catherine *sensing now an imperious demand, turns with some fear, with a discovery, to* **Beatrice**. *She is at the edge of tears, as though a familiar world had shattered.*

Catherine   Okay.

Lights out on them and up on **Alfieri**, *seated behind his desk.*

Alfieri It was at this time that he first came to me. I had represented his father in an accident case some years before, and I was acquainted with the family in a casual way. I remember him now as he walked through my doorway –

*Enter **Eddie** down right ramp.*

His eyes were like tunnels; my first thought was that he had committed a crime. [**Eddie** *sits beside the desk, cap in hand, looking out.*]

But soon I saw it was only a passion that had moved into his body, like a stranger. [**Alfieri** *pauses, looks down at his desk, then to **Eddie** as though he were continuing a conversation with him.*] I don't quite understand what I can do for you. Is there a question of law somewhere?

Eddie That's what I want to ask you.

Alfieri Because there's nothing illegal about a girl falling in love with an immigrant.

Eddie Yeah, but what about it if the only reason for it is to get his papers?

Alfieri First of all you don't know that.

Eddie I see it in his eyes; he's laughin' at her and he's laughin' at me.

Alfieri Eddie, I'm a lawyer. I can only deal in what's provable. You understand that, don't you? Can you prove that?

Eddie I know what's in his mind, Mr. Alfieri!

Alfieri Eddie, even if you could prove that –

Eddie Listen… will you listen to me a minute? My father always said you was a smart man. I want you to listen to me.

Alfieri I'm only a lawyer, Eddie.

Eddie Will you listen a minute? I'm talkin' about the law. Lemme just bring out what I mean. A man, which he comes into the country illegal, don't it stand to reason he's gonna take every penny and put it in the sock? Because they don't know from one day to another, right?

Alfieri   All right.

Eddie   He's spendin'. Records he buys now. Shoes. Jackets. Y'understand me? This guy ain't worried. This guy is *here*. So it must be that he's got it all laid out in his mind already – he's stayin'. Right?

Alfieri   Well? What about it?

Eddie   All right. *[He glances at* **Alfieri**, *then down to the floor.]* I'm talking to you confidential, ain't I?

Alfieri   Certainly.

Eddie   I mean it don't go no place but here. Because I don't like to say this about anybody. Even my wife I didn't exactly say this.

Alfieri   What is it?

Eddie   *[Takes a breath and glances briefly over each shoulder]* The guy ain't right, Mr. Alfieri.

Alfieri   What do you mean?

Eddie   I mean he ain't right.

Alfieri   I don't get you.

Eddie   *[Shifts to another position in the chair]* Dja ever get a look at him?

Alfieri   Not that I know of, no.

Eddie   He's a blond guy. Like… platinum. You know what I mean?

Alfieri   No.

Eddie   I mean if you close the paper fast – you could blow him over.

Alfieri   Well that doesn't mean –

Eddie	Wait a minute, I'm tellin' you sump'm. He sings, see. Which is – I mean it's all right, but sometimes he hits a note, see. I turn around. I mean high. You know what I mean?
Alfieri	Well, that's a tenor.
Eddie	I know a tenor, Mr. Alfieri. This ain't no tenor. I mean if you came in the house and you didn't know who was singin', you wouldn't be lookin' for him you be lookin' for her.
Alfieri	Yes, but that's not –
Eddie	I'm tellin' you sump'm, wait a minute. Please, Mr. Alfieri. I'm tryin' to bring out my thoughts here. Couple of nights ago my niece brings out a dress which it's too small for her, because she shot up like a light this last year. He takes the dress, lays it on the table, he cuts it up; one-two-three, he makes a new dress. I mean he looked so sweet there, like an angel – you could kiss him he was so sweet.
Alfieri	Now look, Eddie –
Eddie	Mr. Alfieri, they're laughin' at him on the piers. I'm ashamed. Paper Doll they call him. Blondie now. His brother thinks it's because he's got a sense of humor, see – which he's got – but that ain't what they're laughin'. Which they're not goin' to come out with it because they know he's my relative, which they have to see me if they make a crack, y'know? But I know what they're laughin' at, and when I think of that guy layin' his hands on her I could – I mean it's eatin' me out, Mr. Alfieri, because I struggled for that girl. And now he comes in my house and –
Alfieri	Eddie, look – I have my own children. I understand you. But the law is very specific. The law does not…
Eddie	*[With a fuller flow of indignation]* You mean to tell me that there's no law that a guy which he ain't right can go to work and marry a girl and – ?
Alfieri	You have no recourse in the law, Eddie.
Eddie	Yeah, but if he ain't right, Mr. Alfieri, you mean to tell me –

Alfieri   There is nothing you can do, Eddie, believe me.

Eddie   Nothin'.

Alfieri   Nothing at all. There's only one legal question here.

Eddie   What?

Alfieri   The manner in which they entered the country. But I don't think you want to do anything about that, do you?

Eddie   You mean – ?

Alfieri   Well, they entered illegally.

Eddie   Oh, Jesus, no, I wouldn't do nothin' about that, I mean –

Alfieri   All right, then, let me talk now, eh?

Eddie   Mr. Alfieri, I can't believe what you tell me. I mean there must be some kinda law which –

Alfieri   Eddie, I want you to listen to me. *[Pause]* You know, sometimes God mixes up the people. We all love somebody, the wife, the kids – every man's got somebody that he loves, heh? But sometimes… there's too much. You know? There's too much, and it goes where it mustn't. A man works hard, he brings up a child, sometimes it's a niece, sometimes even a daughter, and he never realizes it, but through the years – there is too much love for the daughter, there is too much love for the niece. Do you understand what I'm saying to you?

Eddie   *[Sardonically]* What do you mean, I shouldn't look out for her good?

Alfieri   Yes, but these things have to end, Eddie, that's all. The child has to grow up and go away, and the man has to learn to forget. Because after all, Eddie – what other way can it end? *[Pause]* Let her go. That's my advice. You did your job, now it's her life; wish her luck, and let her go. *[Pause]* Will you do that? Because there's no law, Eddie; make up your mind to it; the law is not interested in this.

Eddie You mean to tell me, even if he's a punk? If he's –

Alfieri There's nothing you can do.

Eddie stands.

Eddie Well, all right, thanks. Thanks very much.

Alfieri What are you going to do?

Eddie [With a helpless but ironic gesture] What can I do? I'm a patsy, what can a patsy do? I worked like a dog twenty years so a punk could have her, so that's what I done. I mean, in the worst times, in the worst, when there wasn't a ship comin' in the harbor, I didn't stand around lookin' for relief – I hustled. When there was empty piers in Brooklyn I went to Hoboken, Staten Island, the West Side, Jersey, all over – because I made a promise. I took out of my own mouth to give to her. I took out of my wife's mouth. I walked hungry plenty days in this city! [It begins to break through.] And now I gotta sit in my own house and look at a son-of-a-bitch punk like that – which he came out of nowhere! I give him my house to sleep! I take the blankets off my bed for him, and he takes and puts his dirty filthy hands on her like a goddam thief!

Alfieri [Rising] But, Eddie, she's a woman now.

Eddie He's stealing from me!

Alfieri She wants to get married, Eddie. She can't marry you, can she?

Eddie [Furiously] What're you talkin' about, marry me! I don't know what the hell you're talkin' about!

Pause.

Alfieri I gave you my advice, Eddie. That's it.

Eddie gathers himself. A pause.

Eddie Well, thanks. Thanks very much. It just – it's breakin' my heart, y'know. I –

Alfieri I understand. Put it out of your mind. Can you do that?

Eddie I'm – *[He feels the threat of sobs, and with a helpless wave]* I'll see you around. *[He goes out up the right ramp.]*

Alfieri *[Sits on desk]* There are times when you want to spread an alarm, but nothing has happened. I knew, I knew then and there – I could have finished the whole story that afternoon. It wasn't as though there was a mystery to unravel. I could see every step coming, step after step, like a dark figure walking down a hall toward a certain door. I knew where he was heading for, I knew where he was going to end. And I sat here many afternoons asking myself why, being an intelligent man, I was so powerless to stop it. I even went to a certain old lady in the neighborhood, a very wise old woman, and I told her, and she only nodded, and said, 'Pray for him…' And so I – waited here.

As lights go out on **Alfieri**, *they rise in the apartment where all are finishing dinner.* **Beatrice** *and* **Catherine** *are clearing the table.*

Catherine You know where they went?

Beatrice Where?

Catherine They went to Africa once. On a fishing boat. *[Eddie glances at her.]* It's true, Eddie.

Beatrice *exits into the kitchen with dishes.*

Eddie I didn't say nothin'. *[He goes to his rocker, picks up a newspaper.]*

Catherine And I was never even in Staten Island.

Eddie *[Sitting with the paper]* You didn't miss nothin'. *[Pause.* **Catherine** *takes dishes out.]* How long that take you, Marco – to get to Africa?

Marco *[Rising]* Oh… two days. We go all over.

Rodolpho *[Rising]* Once we went to Yugoslavia.

Eddie *[To* **Marco***]* They pay all right on them boats?

Beatrice *enters. She and* **Rodolpho** *stack the remaining dishes.*

Marco	If they catch fish they pay all right. *[Sits on a stool]*
Rodolpho	They're family boats, though. And nobody in our family owned one. So we only worked when one of the families was sick.
Beatrice	Y'know, Marco, what I don't understand – there's an ocean full of fish and yiz are all starvin'.
Eddie	They gotta have boats, nets, you need money.

Catherine *enters.*

Beatrice	Yeah, but couldn't they like fish from the beach? You see them down Coney Island –
Marco	Sardines.
Eddie	Sure. *[Laughing]* How you gonna catch sardines on a hook?
Beatrice	Oh, I didn't know they're sardines. *[To* **Catherine***]* They're sardines!
Catherine	Yeah, they follow them all over the ocean, Africa, Yugoslavia… *[She sits and begins to look through a movie magazine.* **Rodolpho** *joins her.]*
Beatrice	*[To* **Eddie***]* It's funny, y'know. You never think of it, that sardines are swimming in the ocean! *[She exits to kitchen with dishes.]*
Catherine	I know. It's like oranges and lemons on a tree. *[To* **Eddie***]* I mean you ever think of oranges and lemons on a tree?
Eddie	Yeah, I know. It's funny. *[To* **Marco***]* I heard that they paint the oranges to make them look orange.

Beatrice *enters.*

Marco	*[He has been reading a letter.]* Paint?
Eddie	Yeah, I heard that they grow like green.
Marco	No, in Italy the oranges are orange.

Rodolpho	Lemons are green.
Eddie	*[Resenting his instruction]* I know lemons are green, for Christ's sake, you see them in the store they're green sometimes. I said oranges they paint, I didn't say nothin' about lemons.
Beatrice	*[Sitting; diverting their attention]* Your wife is gettin' the money all right, Marco?
Marco	Oh, yes. She bought medicine for my boy.
Beatrice	That's wonderful. You feel better, heh?
Marco	Oh, yes! But I'm lonesome.
Beatrice	I just hope you ain't gonna do like some of them around here. They're here twenty-five years, some men, and they didn't get enough together to go back twice.
Marco	Oh, I know. We have many families in our town, the children never saw the father. But I will go home. Three, four years, I think.
Beatrice	Maybe you should keep more here. Because maybe she thinks it comes so easy you'll never get ahead of yourself.
Marco	Oh, no, she saves. I send everything. My wife is very lonesome. *[He smiles shyly.]*
Beatrice	She must be nice. She pretty? I bet, heh?
Marco	*[Blushing]* No, but she understand everything.
Rodolpho	Oh, he's got a clever wife!
Eddie	I betcha there's plenty surprises sometimes when those guys get back there, heh?
Marco	Surprises?
Eddie	*[Laughing]* I mean, you know – they count the kids and there's a couple extra than when they left?
Marco	No – no... The women wait, Eddie. Most. Most. Very few surprises.

Rodolpho	It's more strict in our town. [**Eddie** *looks at him now.*] It's not so free.
Eddie	[*Rises, paces up and down*] It ain't so free here either, Rodolpho, like you think. I seen greenhorns sometimes get in trouble that way – they think just because a girl don't go around with a shawl over her head that she ain't strict, y'know? Girl don't have to wear black dress to be strict. Know what I mean?
Rodolpho	Well, I always have respect –
Eddie	I know, but in your town you wouldn't just drag off some girl without permission, I mean. [*He turns.*] You know what I mean, Marco? It ain't that much different here.
Marco	[*Cautiously*] Yes.
Beatrice	Well, he didn't exactly drag her off though, Eddie.
Eddie	I know, but I seen some of them get the wrong idea sometimes. [*To* **Rodolpho**] I mean it might be a little more free here but it's just as strict.
Rodolpho	I have respect for her, Eddie. I do anything wrong?
Eddie	Look, kid, I ain't her father, I'm only her uncle –
Beatrice	Well then, be an uncle then. [**Eddie** *looks at her, aware of her criticizing force.*] I mean.
Marco	No, Beatrice, if he does wrong you must tell him. [*To* **Eddie**] What does he do wrong?
Eddie	Well, Marco, till he came here she was never out on the street twelve o'clock at night.
Marco	[*To* **Rodolpho**] You come home early now.
Beatrice	[*To* **Catherine**] Well, you said the movie ended late, didn't you?
Catherine	Yeah.
Beatrice	Well, tell him, honey. [*To* **Eddie**] The movie ended late.
Eddie	Look, B., I'm just sayin' – he thinks she always stayed out like that.

Marco	You come home early now, Rodolpho.
Rodolpho	*[Embarrassed]* All right, sure. But I can't stay in the house all the time, Eddie.
Eddie	Look, kid, I'm not only talkin' about her. The more you run around like that the more chance you're takin'. *[To **Beatrice**]* I mean suppose he gets hit by a car or something. *[To **Marco**]* Where's his papers, who is he? Know what I mean?
Beatrice	Yeah, but who is he in the daytime, though? It's the same chance in the daytime.
Eddie	*[Holding back a voice full of anger]* Yeah, but he don't have to go lookin' for it, Beatrice. If he's here to work, then he should work; if he's here for a good time then he could fool around! *[To **Marco**]* But I understood, Marco, that you was both comin' to make a livin' for your family. You understand me, don't you, Marco? *[He goes to his rocker.]*
Marco	I beg your pardon, Eddie.
Eddie	I mean, that's what I understood in the first place, see.
Marco	Yes. That's why we came.
Eddie	*[Sits on his rocker]* Well, that's all I'm askin'.
	Eddie *reads his paper. There is a pause, an awkwardness. Now* **Catherine** *gets up and puts a record on the phonograph – 'Paper Doll'.*
Catherine	*[Flushed with revolt]* You wanna dance, Rodolpho?
	Eddie *freezes.*
Rodolpho	*[In deference to **Eddie**]* No, I – I'm tired.
Beatrice	Go ahead, dance, Rodolpho.
Catherine	Ah, come on. They got a beautiful quartet, these guys. Come.
	She has taken his hand and he stiffly rises, feeling **Eddie's** *eyes on his back, and they dance.*

Eddie	*[To Catherine]* What's that, a new record?
Catherine	It's the same one. We bought it the other day.
Beatrice	*[To Eddie]* They only bought three records. *[She watches them dance.* **Eddie** *turns his head away.* **Marco** *just sits there, waiting. Now* **Beatrice** *turns to* **Eddie**.*]* Must be nice to go all over in one of them fishin' boats. I would like that myself. See all them other countries?
Eddie	Yeah.
Beatrice	*[To Marco]* But the women don't go along, I bet.
Marco	No, not on the boats. Hard work.
Beatrice	What're you got, a regular kitchen and everything?
Marco	Yes, we eat very good on the boats – especially when Rodolpho comes along; everybody gets fat.
Beatrice	Oh, he cooks?
Marco	Sure, very good cook. Rice, pasta, fish, everything.
	Eddie *lowers his paper.*
Eddie	He's a cook, too! *[Looking at* **Rodolpho**] He sings, he cooks…
	Rodolpho *smiles thankfully.*
Beatrice	Well it's good, he could always make a living.
Eddie	It's wonderful. He sings, he cooks, he could make dresses…
Catherine	They get some high pay, them guys. The head chefs in all the big hotels are men. You read about them.
Eddie	That's what I'm sayin'.
	Catherine *and* **Rodolpho** *continue dancing.*
Catherine	Yeah, well, I mean.
Eddie	*[To Beatrice]* He's lucky, believe me. *[Slight pause. He looks away, then back to* **Beatrice**.*]* That's why the waterfront is no place for him. *[They*

stop dancing. **Rodolpho** *turns off phonograph.]* I mean like me – I can't cook, I can't sing, I can't make dresses, so I'm on the waterfront. But if I could cook, if I could sing, if I could make dresses, I wouldn't be on the waterfront. *[He has been unconsciously twisting the newspaper into a tight roll. They are all regarding him now; he senses he is exposing the issue and he is driven on.]* I would be someplace else. I would be like in a dress store. *[He has bent the rolled paper and it suddenly tears in two. He suddenly gets up and pulls his pants up over his belly and goes to* **Marco**.*]* What do you say, Marco, we go to the bouts next Saturday night. You never seen a fight, did you?

Marco	*[Uneasily]* Only in the moving pictures.
Eddie	*[Going to* **Rodolpho***]* I'll treat yiz. What do you say, Danish? You wanna come along? I'll buy the tickets.
Rodolpho	Sure. I like to go.
Catherine	*[Goes to* **Eddie***; nervously happy now]* I'll make some coffee, all right?
Eddie	Go ahead, make some! Make it nice and strong. *[Mystified, she smiles and exits to kitchen. He is weirdly elated, rubbing his fists into his palms. He strides to* **Marco**.*]* You wait, Marco, you see some real fights here. You ever do any boxing?
Marco	No, I never.
Eddie	*[To* **Rodolpho***]* Betcha you have done some, heh?
Rodolpho	No.
Eddie	Well, come on, I'll teach you.
Beatrice	What's he got to learn that for?
Eddie	Ya can't tell, one a these days somebody's liable to step on his foot or sump'm. Come on, Rodolpho, I show you a couple a passes. *[He stands below table.]*
Beatrice	Go ahead, Rodolpho. He's a good boxer, he could teach you.
Rodolpho	*[Embarrassed]* Well, I don't know how to – *[He moves down to* **Eddie**.*]*

55

Eddie	Just put your hands up. Like this, see? That's right. That's very good, keep your left up, because you lead with the left, see, like this. *[He gently moves his left into* **Rodolpho's** *face.]* See? Now what you gotta do is you gotta block me, so when I come in like that you – *[* **Rodolpho** *parries his left.]* Hey, that's very good! *[* **Rodolpho** *laughs.]* All right, now come into me. Come on.
Rodolpho	I don't want to hit you, Eddie.
Eddie	Don't pity me, come on. Throw it, I'll show you how to block it. *[* **Rodolpho** *jabs at him, laughing. The others join.]* 'At's it. Come on again. For the jaw right here. *[* **Rodolpho** *jabs with more assurance.]* Very good!
Beatrice	*[To* **Marco** *]* He's very good!

Eddie *crosses directly upstage of* **Rodolpho.**

Eddie	Sure, he's great! Come on, kid, put sump'm behind it, you can't hurt me. *[* **Rodolpho,** *more seriously, jabs at* **Eddie's** *jaw and grazes it.]* Attaboy.

Catherine *comes from the kitchen, watches.*

Now I'm gonna hit you, so block me, see?

Catherine	*[With beginning alarm]* What are they doin'?

They are lightly boxing now.

Beatrice	*[She senses only the comradeship in it now.]* He's teachin' him; he's very good!
Eddie	Sure, he's terrific! Look at him go! *[* **Rodolpho** *lands a blow.]* 'At's it! Now, watch out, here I come, Danish! *[He feints with his left hand and lands with his right. It mildly staggers* **Rodolpho.** **Marco** *rises.]*
Catherine	*[Rushing to* **Rodolpho** *]* Eddie!
Eddie	Why? I didn't hurt him. Did I hurt you, kid? *[He rubs the back of his hand across his mouth.]*

Rodolpho	No, no, he didn't hurt me. *[To* **Eddie** *with a certain gleam and a smile]* I was only surprised.
Beatrice	*[Pulling* **Eddie** *down into the rocker]* That's enough, Eddie; he did pretty good, though.
Eddie	Yeah. *[Rubbing his fists together]* He could be very good, Marco. I'll teach him again.

Marco *nods at him dubiously.*

Rodolpho	Dance, Catherine. Come. *[He takes her hand; they go to the phonograph and start it. It plays 'Paper Doll'.]*

Rodolpho *takes her in his arms. They dance.* **Eddie** *in thought sits in his chair, and* **Marco** *takes a chair, places it in front of* **Eddie**, *and looks down at it.* **Beatrice** *and* **Eddie** *watch him.*

Marco	Can you lift this chair?
Eddie	What do you mean?
Marco	From here. *[He gets on one knee with one hand behind his back, and grasps the bottom of one of the chair legs but does not raise it.]*
Eddie	Sure, why not? *[He comes to the chair, kneels, grasps the leg, raises the chair one inch, but it leans over to the floor.]* Gee, that's hard, I never knew that. *[He tries again, and again fails.]* It's on an angle, that's why, heh?
Marco	Here. *[He kneels, grasps, and with strain slowly raises the chair higher and higher, getting to his feet now.* **Rodolpho** *and* **Catherine** *have stopped dancing as* **Marco** *raises the chair over his head.]*

Marco *is face to face with* **Eddie**, *a strained tension gripping his eyes and jaw, his neck stiff, the chair raised like a weapon over* **Eddie's** *head – and he transforms what might appear like a glare of warning into a smile of triumph, and* **Eddie's** *grin vanishes as he absorbs his look.*

CURTAIN

ACT TWO

*Light rises on **Alfieri** at his desk.*

Alfieri On the twenty-third of that December a case of Scotch whisky slipped from a net while being unloaded – as a case of Scotch whisky is inclined to do on the twenty-third of December on Pier Forty-one. There was no snow, but it was cold, his wife was out shopping. Marco was still at work. The boy had not been hired that day; Catherine told me later that this was the first time they had been alone together in the house.

*Light is rising on **Catherine** in the apartment. **Rodolpho** is watching as she arranges a paper pattern on cloth spread on the table.*

Catherine You hungry?

Rodolpho Not for anything to eat. *[Pause]* I have nearly three hundred dollars. Catherine?

Catherine I heard you.

Rodolpho You don't like to talk about it anymore?

Catherine Sure, I don't mind talkin' about it.

Rodolpho What worries you, Catherine?

Catherine I been wantin' to ask you about something. Could I?

Rodolpho All the answers are in my eyes, Catherine. But you don't look in my eyes lately. You're full of secrets. *[She looks at him. She seems withdrawn.]* What is the question?

Catherine Suppose I wanted to live in Italy.

Rodolpho *[Smiling at the incongruity]* You going to marry somebody rich?

Catherine No, I mean live there – you and me.

Rodolpho	*[His smile vanishing]* When?
Catherine	Well… when we get married.
Rodolpho	*[Astonished]* You want to be an Italian?
Catherine	No, but I could live there without being Italian. Americans live there.
Rodolpho	Forever?
Catherine	Yeah.
Rodolpho	*[Crosses to the rocker]* You're fooling.
Catherine	No, I mean it.
Rodolpho	Where do you get such an idea?
Catherine	Well, you're always saying it's so beautiful there, with the mountains and the ocean and all the –
Rodolpho	You're fooling me.
Catherine	I mean it.
Rodolpho	*[Goes to her slowly]* Catherine, if I ever brought you home with no money, no business, nothing, they would call the priest and the doctor and they would say Rodolpho is crazy.
Catherine	I know, but I think we would be happier there.
Rodolpho	Happier! What would you eat? You can't cook the view!
Catherine	Maybe you could be a singer, like in Rome or –
Rodolpho	Rome! Rome is full of singers.
Catherine	Well, I could work then.
Rodolpho	Where?
Catherine	God, there must be jobs somewhere!

Rodolpho	There's nothing! Nothing, nothing, nothing. Now tell me what you're talking about. How can I bring you from a rich country to suffer in a poor country? What are you talking about? *[She searches for words.]* I would be a criminal stealing your face. In two years you would have an old, hungry face. When my brother's babies cry they give them water, water that boiled a bone. Don't you believe that?
Catherine	*[Quietly]* I'm afraid of Eddie here.
	Slight pause.
Rodolpho	*[Steps closer to her]* We wouldn't live here. Once I am a citizen I could work anywhere and I would find better jobs and we would have a house, Catherine. If I were not afraid to be arrested I would start to be something wonderful here!
Catherine	*[Steeling herself]* Tell me something. I mean just tell me, Rodolpho – would you still want to do it if it turned out we had to go live in Italy? I mean just if it turned out that way.
Rodolpho	This is your question or his question?
Catherine	I would like to know, Rodolpho. I mean it.
Rodolpho	To go there with nothing.
Catherine	Yeah.
Rodolpho	No. *[She looks at him wide-eyed.]* No.
Catherine	You wouldn't?
Rodolpho	No; I will not marry you to live in Italy. I want you to be my wife, and I want to be a citizen. Tell him that, or I will. Yes. *[He moves about angrily.]* And tell him also, and tell yourself, please, that I am not a beggar, and you are not a horse, a gift, a favor for a poor immigrant.
Catherine	Well, don't get mad!
Rodolpho	I am furious! *[Goes to her]* Do you think I am so desperate? My brother is desperate, not me. You think I would carry on my back the rest of my

life a woman I didn't love just to be an American? It's so wonderful? You think we have no tall buildings in Italy? Electric lights? No wide streets? No flags? No automobiles? Only work we don't have. I want to be an American so I can work, that is the only wonder here – work! How can you insult me, Catherine?

Catherine   I didn't mean that –

Rodolpho   My heart dies to look at you. Why are you so afraid of him?

Catherine   *[Near tears]* I don't know!

Rodolpho   Do you trust me, Catherine? You?

Catherine   It's only that I – He was good to me, Rodolpho. You don't know him; he was always the sweetest guy to me. Good. He razzes me all the time but he don't mean it. I know. I would – just feel ashamed if I made him sad. 'Cause I always dreamt that when I got married he would be happy at the wedding, and laughin' – and now he's – mad all the time and nasty – *[She is weeping.]* Tell him you'd live in Italy – just tell him, and maybe he would start to trust you a little, see? Because I want him to be happy; I mean – I like him, Rodolpho – and I can't stand it!

Rodolpho   Oh, Catherine – oh, little girl.

Catherine   I love you, Rodolpho, I love you.

Rodolpho   Then why are you afraid? That he'll spank you?

Catherine   Don't, don't laugh at me! I've been here all my life... Every day I saw him when he left in the morning and when he came home at night. You think it's so easy to turn around and say to a man he's nothin' to you no more?

Rodolpho   I know, but –

Catherine   You don't know; nobody knows! I'm not a baby, I know a lot more than people think I know. Beatrice says to be a woman, but –

Rodolpho   Yes.

Catherine	Then why don't she be a woman? If I was a wife I would make a man happy instead of goin' at him all the time. I can tell a block away when he's blue in his mind and just wants to talk to somebody quiet and nice... I can tell when he's hungry or wants a beer before he even says anything. I know when his feet hurt him, I mean I know him and now I'm supposed to turn around and make a stranger out of him? I don't know why I have to do that, I mean.
Rodolpho	Catherine. If I take in my hands a little bird. And she grows and wishes to fly. But I will not let her out of my hands because I love her so much, is that right for me to do? I don't say you must hate him; but anyway you must go, mustn't you? Catherine?
Catherine	[Softly] Hold me.
Rodolpho	[Clasping her to him] Oh, my little girl.
Catherine	Teach me. [She is weeping.] I don't know anything, teach me, Rodolpho, hold me.
Rodolpho	There's nobody here now. Come inside. Come. [He is leading her toward the bedrooms.] And don't cry any more.
	*Light rises on the street. In a moment **Eddie** appears. He is unsteady, drunk. He mounts the stairs. He enters the apartment, looks around, takes out a bottle from one pocket, puts it on the table. Then another bottle from another pocket, and a third from an inside pocket. He sees the pattern and cloth, goes over to it and touches it, and turns toward upstage.*
Eddie	Beatrice? [He goes to the open kitchen door and looks in.] Beatrice? Beatrice?
	***Catherine** enters from bedroom; under his gaze she adjusts her dress.*
Catherine	You got home early.
Eddie	Knocked off for Christmas early. [Indicating the pattern] Rodolpho makin' you a dress?
Catherine	No. I'm makin' a blouse.

Rodolpho appears in the bedroom doorway. **Eddie** *sees him and his arm jerks slightly in shock.* **Rodolpho** *nods to him testingly.*

Rodolpho Beatrice went to buy presents for her mother.

Pause.

Eddie Pack it up. Go ahead. Get your stuff and get outa here. *[***Catherine*** *instantly turns and walks toward the bedroom, and* **Eddie** *grabs her arm.]* Where you goin'?

Catherine *[Trembling with fright]* I think I have to get out of here, Eddie.

Eddie No, you ain't goin' nowhere, he's the one.

Catherine I think I can't stay here no more. *[She frees her arm, steps back toward the bedroom.]* I'm sorry, Eddie. *[She sees the tears in his eyes.]* Well, don't cry. I'll be around the neighborhood; I'll see you. I just can't stay here no more. You know I can't. *[Her sobs of pity and love for him break her composure.]* Don't you know I can't? You know that, don't you? *[She goes to him.]* Wish me luck. *[She clasps her hands prayerfully.]* Oh, Eddie, don't be like that!

Eddie You ain't goin' nowheres.

Catherine Eddie, I'm not gonna be a baby anymore! You –

He reaches out suddenly, draws her to him, and as she strives to free herself he kisses her on the mouth.

Rodolpho Don't! *[He pulls on* **Eddie's** *arm.]* Stop that! Have respect for her!

Eddie *[Spun round by* **Rodolpho***]* You want something?

Rodolpho Yes! She'll be my wife. That is what I want. My wife!

Eddie But what're you gonna be?

Rodolpho I show you what I be!

Catherine Wait outside; don't argue with him!

Eddie   Come on, show me! What're you gonna be? Show me!

Rodolpho   *[With tears of rage]* Don't say that to me!

Rodolpho flies at him in attack. Eddie pins his arms, laughing, and suddenly kisses him.

Catherine   Eddie! Let go, ya hear me! I'll kill you! Leggo of him!

She tears at Eddie's face and Eddie releases Rodolpho. Eddie stands there with tears rolling down his face as he laughs mockingly at Rodolpho. She is staring at him in horror. Rodolpho is rigid. They are like animals that have torn at one another and broken up without a decision, each waiting for the other's mood.

Eddie   *[To Catherine]* You see? *[To Rodolpho]* I give you till tomorrow, kid. Get outa here. Alone. You hear me? Alone.

Catherine   I'm going with him, Eddie. *[She starts toward Rodolpho.]*

Eddie   *[Indicating Rodolpho with his head]* Not with that.

[She halts, frightened. He sits, still panting for breath, and they watch him helplessly as he leans toward them over the table.] Don't make me do nuttin', Catherine. Watch your step, submarine. By rights they oughta throw you back in the water. But I got pity for you. *[He moves unsteadily toward the door, always facing Rodolpho.]* Just get outa here and don't lay another hand on her unless you wanna go out feet first. *[He goes out of the apartment.]*

The lights go down, as they rise on Alfieri.

Alfieri   On December twenty-seventh I saw him next. I normally go home well before six, but that day I sat around looking out my window at the bay, and when I saw him walking through my doorway, I knew why I had waited. And if I seem to tell this like a dream, it was that way. Several moments arrived in the course of the two talks we had when it occurred to me how – almost transfixed I had come to feel. I had lost my strength somewhere. *[Eddie enters, removing his cap, sits in the chair, looks thoughtfully out.]* I looked in his eyes more than I listened – in fact, I can hardly remember the conversation. But I will never forget how dark the room became when he looked at me; his eyes were like tunnels. I kept wanting to call the police, but nothing had happened. Nothing at all had really happened. *[He breaks off and looks down at the desk. Then he turns to* **Eddie**.*]* So in other words, he won't leave?

Eddie My wife is talkin' about renting a room upstairs for them. An old lady on the top floor is got an empty room.

Alfieri What does Marco say?

Eddie He just sits there. Marco don't say much.

Alfieri I guess they didn't tell him, heh? What happened?

Eddie I don't know; Marco don't say much.

Alfieri What does your wife say?

Eddie *[Unwilling to pursue this]* Nobody's talkin' much in the house. So what about that?

Alfieri But you didn't prove anything about him. It sounds like he just wasn't strong enough to break your grip.

Eddie I'm tellin' you I know – he ain't right. Somebody that don't want it can break it. Even a mouse, if you catch a teeny mouse and you hold it in your hand, that mouse can give you the right kind of fight. He didn't give me the right kind of fight, I know it, Mr. Alfieri, the guy ain't right.

Alfieri What did you do that for, Eddie?

Eddie To show her what he is! So she would see, once and for all! Her mother'll turn over in the grave! *[He gathers himself almost peremptorily.]* So what do I gotta do now? Tell me what to do.

Alfieri She actually said she's marrying him?

Eddie She told me, yeah. So what do I do?

Slight pause.

Alfieri   This is my last word, Eddie, take it or not, that's your business. Morally and legally you have no rights, you cannot stop it; she is a free agent.

Eddie   *[Angering]* Didn't you hear what I told you?

Alfieri   *[With a tougher tone]* I heard what you told me, and I'm telling you what the answer is. I'm not only telling you now, I'm warning you – the law is nature. The law is only a word for what has a right to happen. When the law is wrong it's because it's unnatural, but in this case it is natural and a river will drown you if you buck it now. Let her go. And bless her. *[A phone booth begins to glow on the opposite side of the stage; a faint, lonely blue.* **Eddie** *stands up, jaws clenched.]* Somebody had to come for her, Eddie, sooner or later. *[***Eddie** *starts turning to go and Alfieri rises with new anxiety.]* You won't have a friend in the world, Eddie! Even those who understand will turn against you, even the ones who feel the same will despise you! *[***Eddie** *moves off.]* Put it out of your mind! Eddie! *[He follows into the darkness, calling desperately.]*

Eddie is gone. The phone is glowing in light now. Light is out on **Alfieri**. **Eddie** *has at the same time appeared beside the phone.*

Eddie   Give me the number of the Immigration Bureau. Thanks. *[He dials.]* I want to report something. Illegal immigrants. Two of them. That's right. Four-forty-one Saxon Street, Brooklyn, yeah. Ground floor. Heh? *[With greater difficulty]* I'm just around the neighborhood, that's all. Heh?

Evidently he is being questioned further, and he slowly hangs up. He leaves the phone just as **Louis** *and* **Mike** *come down the street.*

Louis   Go bowlin', Eddie?

Eddie   No, I'm due home.

Louis   Well, take it easy.

Eddie   I'll see yiz.

They leave him, exiting right, and he watches them go. He glances about, then goes up into the house. The lights go on in the apartment. **Beatrice** *is taking down Christmas decorations and packing them in a box.*

Eddie   Where is everybody? *[Beatrice does not answer.]* I says where is everybody?

Beatrice   *[Looking up at him, wearied with it, and concealing a fear of him]* I decided to move them upstairs with Mrs. Dondero.

Eddie   Oh, they're all moved up there already?

Beatrice   Yeah.

Eddie   Where's Catherine? She up there?

Beatrice   Only to bring pillowcases.

Eddie   She ain't movin' in with them.

Beatrice   Look, I'm sick and tired of it. I'm sick and tired of it!

Eddie   All right, all right, take it easy.

Beatrice   I don't wanna hear no more about it, you understand? Nothin'!

Eddie   What're you blowin' off about? Who brought them in here?

Beatrice   All right, I'm sorry; I wish I'd a drop dead before I told them to come. In the ground I wish I was.

Eddie   Don't drop dead, just keep in mind who brought them in here, that's all. *[He moves about restlessly.]* I mean I got a couple of rights here. *[He moves, wanting to beat down her evident disapproval of him.]* This is my house here, not their house.

Beatrice   What do you want from me? They're moved out; what do you want now?

Eddie   I want my respect!

Beatrice   So I moved them out, what more do you want? You got your house now, you got your respect.

Eddie   *[He moves about biting his lip.]* I don't like the way you talk to me, Beatrice.

Beatrice	I'm just tellin' you I done what you want!
Eddie	I don't like it! The way you talk to me and the way you look at me. This is my house. And she is my niece and I'm responsible for her.
Beatrice	So that's why you done that to him?
Eddie	I done what to him?
Beatrice	What you done to him in front of her; you know what I'm talkin' about. She goes around shakin' all the time, she can't go to sleep! That's what you call responsible for her?
Eddie	*[Quietly]* The guy ain't right, Beatrice. *[She is silent.]* Did you hear what I said?
Beatrice	Look, I'm finished with it. That's all. *[She resumes her work.]*
Eddie	*[Helping her to pack the tinsel]* I'm gonna have it out with you one of these days, Beatrice.
Beatrice	Nothin' to have out with me, it's all settled. Now we gonna be like it never happened, that's all.
Eddie	I want my respect, Beatrice, and you know what I'm talkin' about.
Beatrice	What?

Pause.

Eddie	*[Finally his resolution hardens.]* What I feel like doin' in the bed and what I don't feel like doin'. I don't want no –
Beatrice	When'd I say anything about that?
Eddie	You said, you said, I ain't deaf. I don't want no more conversations about that, Beatrice. I do what I feel like doin' or what I don't feel like doin'.
Beatrice	Okay.

Pause.

Eddie   You used to be different, Beatrice. You had a whole different way.

Beatrice   I'm no different.

Eddie   You didn't used to jump me all the time about everything. The last year or two I come in the house I don't know what's gonna hit me. It's a shootin' gallery in here and I'm the pigeon.

Beatrice   Okay, okay.

Eddie   Don't tell me okay, okay, I'm tellin' you the truth. A wife is supposed to believe the husband. If I tell you that guy ain't right don't tell me he is right.

Beatrice   But how do you know?

Eddie   Because I know. I don't go around makin' accusations. He give me the heeby-jeebies the first minute I seen him. And I don't like you sayin' I don't want her marryin' anybody. I broke my back payin' her stenography lessons so she could go out and meet a better class of people. Would I do that if I didn't want her to get married? Sometimes you talk like I was a crazy man or sump'm.

Beatrice   But she likes him.

Eddie   Beatrice, she's a baby, how is she gonna know what she likes?

Beatrice   Well, you kept her a baby, you wouldn't let her go out. I told you a hundred times.

Pause.

Eddie   All right. Let her go out, then.

Beatrice   She don't wanna go out now. It's too late, Eddie.

Pause.

Eddie   Suppose I told her to go out. Suppose I –

Beatrice   They're going to get married next week, Eddie.

Eddie	*[His head jerks around to her.]* She said that?
Beatrice	Eddie, if you want my advice, go to her and tell her good luck. I think maybe now that you had it out you learned better.
Eddie	What's the hurry next week?
Beatrice	Well, she's been worried about him bein' picked up; this way he could start to be a citizen. She loves him, Eddie. *[He gets up, moves about uneasily, restlessly.]* Why don't you give her a good word? Because I still think she would like you to be a friend, y'know? *[He is standing, looking at the floor.]* I mean like if you told her you'd go to the wedding.
Eddie	She asked you that?
Beatrice	I know she would like it. I'd like to make a party here for her. I mean there oughta be some kinda send-off. Heh? I mean she'll have trouble enough in her life, let's start it off happy. What do you say? Cause in her heart she still loves you, Eddie. I know it. *[He presses his fingers against his eyes.]* What're you, cryin'? *[She goes to him, holds his face.]* Go… whyn't you go tell her you're sorry? *[***Catherine*** is seen on the upper landing of the stairway, and they hear her descending.]* There… she's comin' down. Come on, shake hands with her.
Eddie	*[Moving with suppressed suddenness]* No, I can't, I can't talk to her.
Beatrice	Eddie, give her a break; a wedding should be happy!
Eddie	I'm goin', I'm goin' for a walk.
	He goes upstage for his jacket. **Catherine** *enters and starts for the bedroom door.*
Beatrice	Katie?… Eddie, don't go, wait a minute. *[She embraces* **Eddie's** *arm with warmth.]* Ask him, Katie. Come on, honey.
Eddie	It's all right, I'm – *[He starts to go and she holds him.]*
Beatrice	No, she wants to ask you. Come on, Katie, ask him. We'll have a party! What're we gonna do, hate each other? Come on!

Catherine	I'm gonna get married, Eddie. So if you wanna come, the wedding be on Saturday.
	Pause.
Eddie	Okay. I only wanted the best for you, Katie. I hope you know that.
Catherine	Okay. *[She starts out again.]*
Eddie	Catherine? *[She turns to him.]* I was just tellin' Beatrice… if you wanna go out, like… I mean I realize maybe I kept you home too much. Because he's the first guy you ever knew, y'know? I mean now that you got a job, you might meet some fellas, and you get a different idea, y'know? I mean you could always come back to him, you're still only kids, the both of yiz. What's the hurry? Maybe you'll get around a little bit, you grow up a little more, maybe you'll see different in a couple of months. I mean you be surprised, it don't have to be him.
Catherine	No, we made it up already.
Eddie	*[With increasing anxiety]* Katie, wait a minute.
Catherine	No, I made up my mind.
Eddie	But you never knew no other fella, Katie! How could you make up your mind?
Catherine	Cause I did. I don't want nobody else.
Eddie	But, Katie, suppose he gets picked up.
Catherine	That's why we gonna do it right away. Soon as we finish the wedding he's goin' right over and start to be a citizen. I made up my mind, Eddie. I'm sorry. *[To **Beatrice**]* Could I take two more pillowcases for the other guys?
Beatrice	Sure, go ahead. Only don't let her forget where they came from.
	Catherine *goes into a bedroom.*
Eddie	She's got other boarders up there?
Beatrice	Yeah, there's two guys that just came over.

Eddie	What do you mean, came over?
Beatrice	From Italy. Lipari the butcher – his nephew. They come from Bari, they just got here yesterday. I didn't even know till Marco and Rodolpho moved up there before. *[Catherine enters, going toward exit with two pillowcases.]* It'll be nice, they could all talk together.
Eddie	Catherine! *[She halts near the exit door. He takes in Beatrice too.]* What're you, got no brains? You put them up there with two other submarines?
Catherine	Why?
Eddie	*[In a driving fright and anger]* Why! How do you know they're not trackin' these guys? They'll come up for them and find Marco and Rodolpho! Get them out of the house!
Beatrice	But they been here so long already –
Eddie	How do you know what enemies Lipari's got? Which they'd love to stab him in the back?
Catherine	Well what'll I do with them?
Eddie	The neighborhood is full of rooms. Can't you stand to live a couple of blocks away from him? Get them out of the house!
Catherine	Well maybe tomorrow night I'll –
Eddie	Not tomorrow, do it now. Catherine, you never mix yourself with somebody else's family! These guys get picked up, Lipari's liable to blame you or me and we got his whole family on our head. They got a temper, that family.
	Two men in overcoats appear outside, start into the house.
Catherine	How'm I gonna find a place tonight?
Eddie	Will you stop arguin' with me and get them out! You think I'm always tryin' to fool you or sump'm? What's the matter with you, don't you believe I could think of your good? Did I ever ask sump'm for myself?

You think I got no feelin's? I never told you nothin' in my life that wasn't for your good. Nothin'! And look at the way you talk to me! Like I was an enemy! Like I – *[A knock on the door. His head swerves. They all stand motionless. Another knock.* **Eddie**, *in a whisper, pointing upstage.]* Go up the fire escape, get them out over the back fence.

Catherine *stands motionless, uncomprehending.*

First Officer *[In the hall]* Immigration! Open up in there!

Eddie Go, go. Hurry up! *[She stands a moment staring at him in a realized horror.]* Well, what're you lookin' at!

First Officer Open up!

Eddie *[Calling toward door]* Who's that there?

First Officer Immigration, open up.

Eddie *turns, looks at* **Beatrice**. *She sits. Then he looks at* **Catherine**. *With a sob of fury* **Catherine** *streaks into a bedroom.*

Knock is repeated.

Eddie All right, take it easy, take it easy. *[He goes and opens the door.* **First Officer** *steps inside.]* What's all this?

First Officer Where are they?

Second Officer *sweeps past and, glancing about, goes into the kitchen.*

Eddie Where's who?

First Officer Come on, come on, where are they? *[He hurries into the bedrooms.]*

Eddie Who? We got nobody here. *[He looks at* **Beatrice**, *who turns her head away. Pugnaciously, furious, he steps toward* **Beatrice**.*]* What's the matter with you?

First Officer *enters from the bedroom, calls to the kitchen.*

First Officer Dominick?

Enter **Second Officer** *from kitchen.*

Second Officer   Maybe it's a different apartment.

First Officer   There's only two more floors up there. I'll take the front, you go up the fire escape. I'll let you in. Watch your step up there.

Second Officer   Okay, right, Charley. *[***First Officer*** goes out apartment door and runs up the stairs.]* This is Four-forty-one, isn't it?

Eddie   That's right.

Second Officer *goes out into the kitchen.*

Eddie *turns to* **Beatrice**. *She looks at him now and sees his terror.*

Beatrice   *[Weakened with fear]* Oh, Jesus, Eddie.

Eddie   What's the matter with you?

Beatrice   *[Pressing her palms against her face]* Oh, my God, my God.

Eddie   What're you, accusin' me?

Beatrice   *[Her final thrust is to turn toward him instead of running from him.]* My God, what did you do?

Many steps on the outer stair draw his attention. We see **First Officer** *descending, with* **Marco**, *behind him* **Rodolpho**, *and* **Catherine** *and the two strange immigrants, followed by* **Second Officer**. **Beatrice** *hurries to door.*

Catherine   *[Backing down stairs, fighting with* **First Officer**; *as they appear on the stairs]* What do yiz want from them? They work, that's all. They're boarders upstairs, they work on the piers.

Beatrice   *[To* **First Officer***]* Ah, Mister, what do you want from them, who do they hurt?

Catherine   *[Pointing to* **Rodolpho***]* They ain't no submarines, he was born in Philadelphia.

First Officer	Step aside, lady.
Catherine	What do you mean? You can't just come in a house and –
First Officer	All right, take it easy. *[To* **Rodolpho***]* What street were you born in Philadelphia?
Catherine	What do you mean, what street? Could you tell me what street you were born?
First Officer	Sure. Four blocks away, One-eleven Union Street. Let's go fellas.
Catherine	*[Fending him off* **Rodolpho***]* No, you can't! Now, get outa here!
First Officer	Look, girlie, if they're all right they'll be out tomorrow. If they're illegal they go back where they came from. If you want, get yourself a lawyer, although I'm tellin' you now you're wasting your money. Let's get them in the car, Dom. *[To the men]* Andiamo, andiamo, let's go.

The men start, but **Marco** *hangs back.*

Beatrice	*[From doorway]* Who're they hurtin', for God's sake, what do you want from them? They're starvin' over there, what do you want! Marco!

Marco *suddenly breaks from the group and dashes into the room and faces* **Eddie***;* **Beatrice** *and* **First Officer** *rush in as* **Marco** *spits into* **Eddie's** *face.*

Catherine *runs into hallway and throws herself into* **Rodolpho's** *arms.* **Eddie***, with an enraged cry, lunges for* **Marco***.*

Eddie	Oh, you mother's – !

First Officer *quickly intercedes and pushes* **Eddie** *from* **Marco***, who stands there accusingly.*

First Officer	*[Between them, pushing* **Eddie** *from* **Marco***]* Cut it out!
Eddie	*[Over the* **First Officer's** *shoulder, to* **Marco***]* I'll kill you for that, you son of a bitch!
First Officer	Hey! *[Shakes him]* Stay in here now, don't come out, don't bother him. You hear me? Don't come out, fella.

For an instant there is silence. Then **First Officer** *turns and takes* **Marco's** *arm and then gives a last, informative look at* **Eddie***. As he and* **Marco** *are going out into the hall,* **Eddie** *erupts.*

Eddie   I don't forget that, Marco! You hear what I'm sayin'?

Out in the hall, **First Officer** *and* **Marco** *go down the stairs. Now, in the street,* **Louis***,* **Mike** *and several neighbors including the butcher,* **Lipari***, a stout, intense, middle-aged man – are gathering around the stoop.*

Lipari*, the butcher, walks over to the two strange men and kisses them. His wife, keening, goes and kisses their hands.* **Eddie** *is emerging from the house shouting after* **Marco***.* **Beatrice** *is trying to restrain him.*

Eddie   That's the thanks I get? Which I took the blankets off my bed for yiz? You gonna apologize to me, Marco! Marco!

First Officer   *[In the doorway with* **Marco***]* All right, lady, let them go. Get in the car, fellas, it's over there.

Rodolpho *is almost carrying the sobbing* **Catherine** *off up the street, left.*

Catherine   He was born in Philadelphia! What do you want from him?

First Officer   Step aside, lady, come on now…

Second Officer *has moved off with the two strange men.* **Marco***, taking advantage of* **First Officer** *being occupied with* **Catherine***, suddenly frees himself and points back at* **Eddie***.*

Marco   That one! I accuse that one!

Eddie *brushes* **Beatrice** *aside and rushes out to the stoop.*

First Officer   *[Grabbing him and moving him quickly off up the left street]* Come on!

Marco   *[As he is taken off, pointing back at* **Eddie***]* That one! He killed my children! That one stole the food from my children!

Marco *is gone. The crowd has turned to* **Eddie***.*

Eddie	*[To **Lipari** and wife]* He's crazy! I give them the blankets off my bed. Six months I kept them like my own brothers!

Lipari, the butcher, turns and starts up left with his arm around his wife.

Eddie	Lipari! *[He follows **Lipari** up left.]* For Christ's sake, I kept them, I give them the blankets off my bed!

*Lipari and wife exit. **Eddie** turns and starts crossing down right to **Louis** and **Mike**.*

Eddie	Louis! Louis!

*Louis barely turns, then walks off and exits down right with **Mike**. Only Beatrice is left on the stoop. **Catherine** now returns, blank-eyed, from offstage and the car. **Eddie** calls after **Louis** and **Mike**.*

Eddie	He's gonna take that back. He's gonna take that back or I'll kill him! You hear me? I'll kill him! I'll kill him! *[He exits up street calling.]*

*There is a pause of darkness before the lights rise, on the reception room of a prison. **Marco** is seated; **Alfieri**, **Catherine**, and **Rodolpho** standing.*

Alfieri	I'm waiting, Marco, what do you say?
Rodolpho	Marco never hurt anybody.
Alfieri	I can bail you out until your hearing comes up. But I'm not going to do it, you understand me? Unless I have your promise. You're an honorable man, I will believe your promise. Now what do you say?
Marco	In my country he would be dead now. He would not live this long.
Alfieri	All right, Rodolpho – you come with me now.
Rodolpho	No! Please, Mister. Marco – promise the man. Please, I want you to watch the wedding. How can I be married and you're in here? Please, you're not going to do anything; you know you're not.

Marco is silent.

Catherine	*[Kneeling left of Marco]* Marco, don't you understand? He can't bail you out if you're gonna do something bad. To hell with Eddie. Nobody is gonna talk to him again if he lives to a hundred. Everybody knows you spit in his face, that's enough, isn't it? Give me the satisfaction – I want you at the wedding. You got a wife and kids, Marco. You could be workin' till the hearing comes up, instead of layin' around here.
Marco	*[To Alfieri]* I have no chance?
Alfieri	*[Crosses to behind Marco]* No, Marco. You're going back. The hearing is a formality, that's all.
Marco	But him? There is a chance, eh?
Alfieri	When she marries him he can start to become an American. They permit that, if the wife is born here.
Marco	*[Looking at Rodolpho]* Well – we did something. *[He lays a palm on Rodolpho's arm and Rodolpho covers it.]*
Rodolpho	Marco, tell the man.
Marco	*[Pulling his hand away]* What will I tell him? He knows such a promise is dishonorable.
Alfieri	To promise not to kill is not dishonorable.
Marco	*[Looking at Alfieri]* No?
Alfieri	No.
Marco	*[Gesturing with his head – this is a new idea]* Then what is done with such a man?
Alfieri	Nothing. If he obeys the law, he lives. That's all.
Marco	*[Rises, turns to Alfieri]* The law? All the law is not in a book.
Alfieri	Yes. In a book. There is no other law.
Marco	*[His anger rising]* He degraded my brother. My blood. He robbed my children, he mocks my work. I work to come here, mister!

Alfieri	I know, Marco –
Marco	There is no law for that? Where is the law for that?
Alfieri	There is none.
Marco	*[Shaking his head, sitting]* I don't understand this country.
Alfieri	Well? What is your answer? You have five or six weeks you could work. Or else you sit here. What do you say to me?
Marco	*[Lowers his eyes. It almost seems he is ashamed.]* All right.
Alfieri	You won't touch him. This is your promise.

Slight pause.

Marco	Maybe he wants to apologize to me.

Marco *is staring away.* **Alfieri** *takes one of his hands.*

Alfieri	This is not God, Marco. You hear? Only God makes justice.
Marco	All right.
Alfieri	*[Nodding, not with assurance]* Good! Catherine, Rodolpho, Marco, let us go.

Catherine *kisses* **Rodolpho** *and* **Marco**, *then kisses* **Alfieri's** *hand.*

Catherine	I'll get Beatrice and meet you at the church. *[She leaves quickly.]*

Marco *rises.* **Rodolpho** *suddenly embraces him.* **Marco** *pats him on the back and* **Rodolpho** *exits after* **Catherine**. **Marco** *faces* **Alfieri**.

Alfieri	Only God, Marco.

Marco *turns and walks out.* **Alfieri** *with a certain processional tread leaves the stage. The lights dim out.*

The lights rise in the apartment. **Eddie** *is alone in the rocker, rocking back and forth in little surges. Pause. Now* **Beatrice** *emerges from a bedroom. She is in her best clothes, wearing a hat.*

Beatrice	*[With fear, going to **Eddie**]* I'll be back in an hour, Eddie. All right?
Eddie	*[Quietly, almost inaudibly, as though drained]* What, have I been talkin' to myself?
Beatrice	Eddie, for God's sake, it's her wedding.
Eddie	Didn't you hear what I told you? You walk out that door to that wedding you ain't comin' back here, Beatrice.
Beatrice	Why! What do you want?
Eddie	I want my respect. Didn't you ever hear of that? From my wife?
	Catherine *enters from the bedroom.*
Catherine	It's after three; we're supposed to be there already, Beatrice. The priest won't wait.
Beatrice	Eddie. It's her wedding. There'll be nobody there from her family. For my sister let me go. I'm goin' for my sister.
Eddie	*[As though hurt]* Look, I been arguin' with you all day already, Beatrice, and I said what I'm gonna say. He's gonna come here and apologize to me or nobody from this house is goin' into that church today. Now if that's more to you than I am, then go. But don't come back. You be on my side or on their side, that's all.
Catherine	*[Suddenly]* Who the hell do you think you are?
Beatrice	Sssh!
Catherine	You got no more right to tell nobody nothin'! Nobody! The rest of your life, nobody!
Beatrice	Shut up, Katie! *[She turns **Catherine** around.]*
Catherine	You're gonna come with me!
Beatrice	I can't Katie, I can't…

Catherine	How can you listen to him? This rat!
Beatrice	*[Shaking* **Catherine***]* Don't you call him that!
Catherine	*[Clearing from* **Beatrice***]* What're you scared of? He's a rat! He belongs in the sewer!
Beatrice	Stop it!
Catherine	*[Weeping]* He bites people when they sleep! He comes when nobody's lookin' and poisons decent people. In the garbage he belongs!

Eddie *seems about to pick up the table and fling it at her.*

Beatrice	No, Eddie! Eddie! *[To* **Catherine***]* Then we all belong in the garbage. You, and me too. Don't say that. Whatever happened we all done it, and don't you ever forget it, Catherine. *[She goes to* **Catherine***.]* Now go, go to your wedding, Katie, I'll stay home. Go. God bless you, God bless your children.

Enter **Rodolpho**.

Rodolpho	Eddie?
Eddie	Who said you could come in here? Get outa here!
Rodolpho	Marco is coming, Eddie. *[Pause.* **Beatrice** *raises her hands in terror.]* He's praying in the church. You understand? *[Pause.* **Rodolpho** *advances into the room.]* Catherine, I think it is better we go. Come with me.
Catherine	Eddie, go away, please.
Beatrice	*[Quietly]* Eddie. Let's go someplace. Come. You and me. *[He has not moved.]* I don't want you to be here when he comes. I'll get your coat.
Eddie	Where? Where am I goin'? This is my house.
Beatrice	*[Crying out]* What's the use of it! He's crazy now, you know the way they get, what good is it! You got nothin' against Marco, you always liked Marco!

Eddie	I got nothin' against Marco? Which he called me a rat in front of the whole neighbourhood? Which he said I killed his children! Where you been?
Rodolpho	*[Quite suddenly, stepping up to* **Eddie***]* It is my fault, Eddie. Everything. I wish to apologize. It was wrong that I do not ask your permission. I kiss your hand. *[He reaches for* **Eddie's** *hand, but* **Eddie** *snaps it away from him.]*
Beatrice	Eddie, he's apologizing!
Rodolpho	I have made all our troubles. But you have insult me too. Maybe God understand why you did that to me. Maybe you did not mean to insult me at all –
Beatrice	Listen to him! Eddie, listen what he's tellin' you!
Rodolpho	I think, maybe when Marco comes, if we can tell him we are comrades now, and we have no more argument between us. Then maybe Marco will not –
Eddie	Now, listen –
Catherine	Eddie, give him a chance!
Beatrice	What do you want! Eddie, what do you want!
Eddie	I want my name! He didn't take my name; he's only a punk. Marco's got my name – *[To* **Rodolpho***]* and you can run tell him, kid, that he's gonna give it back to me in front of this neighbourhood, or we have it out. *[Hoisting up his pants]* Come on, where is he? Take me to him.
Beatrice	Eddie, listen –
Eddie	I heard enough! Come on, let's go!
Beatrice	Only blood is good? He kissed your hand!
Eddie	What he does don't mean nothin' to nobody! *[To* **Rodolpho***]* Come on!

Beatrice	[Barring his way to the stairs] What's gonna mean somethin'? Eddie, listen to me. Who could give you your name? Listen to me, I love you, I'm talkin' to you, I love you; if Marco'll kiss your hand outside, if he goes on his knees, what is he got to give you? That's not what you want.
Eddie	Don't bother me!
Beatrice	You want somethin' else, Eddie, and you can never have her!
Catherine	[In horror] B.!
Eddie	[Shocked, horrified, his fist clenching] Beatrice!

Marco appears outside, walking toward the door from a distant point.

Beatrice	[Crying out, weeping] The truth is not as bad as blood, Eddie! I'm tellin' you the truth – tell her good-bye forever!
Eddie	[Crying out in agony] That's what you think of me – that I would have such a thought? [His fists clench his head as though it will burst.]
Marco	[Calling near the door outside] Eddie Carbone!

Eddie swerves about; all stand transfixed for an instant. People appear outside.

Eddie	[As though flinging his challenge] Yeah, Marco! Eddie Carbone. Eddie Carbone. Eddie Carbone. [He goes up the stairs and emerges from the apartment. **Rodolpho** streaks up and out past him and runs to **Marco**.]
Rodolpho	No, Marco, please! Eddie, please, he has children! You will kill a family!
Beatrice	Go in the house! Eddie, go in the house!
Eddie	[He gradually comes to address the people.] Maybe he come to apologize to me. Heh, Marco? For what you said about me in front of the neighborhood? [He is incensing himself and little bits of laughter even escape him as his eyes are murderous and he cracks his knuckles in his hands with a strange sort of relaxation.] He knows that ain't right. To do like that? To a man? Which I put my roof over their head and

my food in their mouth? Like in the Bible? Strangers I never seen in my whole life? To come out of the water and grab a girl for a passport? To go and take from your own family like from the stable – and never a word to me? And now accusations in the bargain! *[Directly to* **Marco***]* Wipin' the neighborhood with my name like a dirty rag! I want my name, Marco. *[He is moving now, carefully, toward* **Marco***.]* Now gimme my name and we go together to the wedding.

**Beatrice and
Catherine**   *[Keening]* Eddie! Eddie, don't! Eddie!

Eddie   No, Marco knows what's right from wrong. Tell the people, Marco, tell them what a liar you are! *[He has his arms spread and* **Marco** *is spreading his.]* Come on, liar, you know what you done! *[He lunges for* **Marco** *as a great hushed shout goes up from the people.]*

Marco *strikes* **Eddie** *beside the neck.*

Marco   Animal! You go on your knees to me!

Eddie *goes down with the blow and* **Marco** *starts to raise a foot to stomp him when* **Eddie** *springs a knife into his hand and* **Marco** *steps back.* **Louis** *rushes in toward* **Eddie***.*

Louis   Eddie, for Christ's sake!

Eddie *raises the knife and* **Louis** *halts and steps back.*

Eddie   You lied about me, Marco. Now say it. Come on now, say it!

Marco   Anima-a-a-l!

Eddie *lunges with the knife.* **Marco** *grabs his arm, turning the blade inward and pressing it home as the women and* **Louis** *and* **Mike** *rush in and separate them, and* **Eddie***, the knife still in his hand, falls to his knees before* **Marco***. The two women support him for a moment, calling his name again and again.*

Catherine   Eddie I never meant to do nothing bad to you.

Eddie   Then why – Oh, B.!

Beatrice   Yes, yes!

Eddie   My B.!

He dies in her arms, and **Beatrice** *covers him with her body.* **Alfieri,** *who is in the crowd, turns out to the audience. The lights have gone down, leaving him in a glow, while behind him the dull prayers of the people and the keening of the women continue.*

Alfieri   Most of the time now we settle for half and I like it better. But the truth is holy, and even as I know how wrong he was, and his death useless, I tremble, for I confess that something perversely pure calls to me from his memory – not purely good, but himself purely, for he allowed himself to be wholly known and for that I think I will love him more than all my sensible clients. And yet, it is better to settle for half, it must be! And so I mourn him – I admit it – with a certain… alarm.

CURTAIN

BIOGRAPHY

Arthur Miller was born in New York City in 1915 into a prosperous family of Jewish emigres; his father was a successful manufacturer of ladies' coats. The economic downturn that heralded the Wall Street Crash in 1929 also brought ruin to Miller's father's business; the family moved from their comfortable home in Harlem to a small house in Brooklyn and adapted to a much-diminished style of living.

THE WALL STREET CRASH

The Wall Street Crash of 1929 was the greatest stock market crash in the history of the United States; stock values tumbled, triggering a major financial recession that affected all industrialized countries in the Western world. Millions of businesses were ruined and unemployment in America rose to unprecedented levels.

Miller graduated from high school with disappointing grades and he worked in a warehouse to fund his journalism course at the University of Michigan. Here, Miller began his writing career, winning various awards for his early plays. He later switched from journalism to English literature and took courses in playwriting.

After graduating in 1938, Miller returned to New York and started writing for radio. He married his college girlfriend, Mary Slattery, in 1940 and they moved into a flat in Brooklyn.

In 1944, Miller's first stage play, *The Man Who Had All the Luck*, premiered in New York but closed after only a few performances.

Three years later, Miller had his first major theatrical success with *All My Sons* (1947), directed by Elia Kazan; this was a conventional, 'well-made play', influenced by Miller's study of Ibsen.

Miller also did manual jobs, assembling beer boxes at one point, and for two years during the Second World War he worked nightshifts in the naval dockyard in Brooklyn, where he became familiar with many living examples of the 'common man', who features at the centre of his plays.

In 1947, Miller visited Italy and researched material for a screenplay, *The Hook*, about corruption on the waterfront of New York involving mafia-style gangsterism. Miller and Elia Kazan took the screenplay to Columbia Pictures, which agreed to make the film on condition that Miller made significant changes to the script; Miller refused. Later he made use of his research, to tell the story of Eddie Carbone in *A View from the Bridge*.

Death of a Salesman, also directed by Kazan, was another huge success for Miller in 1949. It attracted many accolades, including six Tony Awards, with Miller being awarded the 1949 Pulitzer Prize for Drama.

Miller's next successful play was *The Crucible* (1953), about the witch trials in Salem, Massachusetts, which offered a thinly veiled attack on the McCarthy 'witch-hunt' of communist party members in the 1950s. The protagonist, John Proctor, like Willy Loman in *Death of a Salesman* and Eddie Carbone to come, represented an ordinary man, decent at heart, prepared to die to protect his name (and, therefore, his reputation) in the manner of a tragic hero.

A View from the Bridge premiered in 1955. The play focused on an ordinary family, thrown into turmoil by the arrival of relatives from Sicily entering America illegally to look for work.

In 1956, Miller, now divorced, married Hollywood star Marilyn Monroe; the marriage did not last, and they divorced in 1961. Miller's 1964 play, *After the Fall*, is generally considered to be based on the disintegration of his marriage to Monroe, who died two years after she and Miller separated.

Arthur Miller's Collected Plays was published with an influential introductory essay by Miller. In 1956, Miller was summoned to appear before the House Un-American Activities Committee (HUAC) to explain his previous association with communist groups.

HOUSE UN-AMERICAN ACTIVITIES COMMITTEE (HUAC)

The House Un-American Activities Committee (HUAC) was a government department that investigated state disloyalty and was both anti-communist and anti-fascist.

Although Miller gave details about his own youthful membership of groups sympathetic to communism, he was convicted of 'contempt of Congress' for refusing to name others who attended such groups. In 1958, Washington's Court of Appeals quashed his conviction after a successful legal battle to clear his name.

Miller dealt with the issue of personal betrayal in *A View from the Bridge*, when Eddie informs the Immigration Bureau of the whereabouts of Rodolpho and Marco, resulting in their arrest.

In 1962, Miller married his third wife Inge Morath, an Austrian photographer.

Miller's later plays, including *Incident at Vichy* (1964), *The Price* (1968) and *Broken Glass* (1994), though not as momentously successful as his earlier plays, only enhanced his reputation as one of the greatest playwrights of the 20th century.

In 1978, *The Theatre Essays of Arthur Miller* was published; his autobiography, *Timebends,* followed in 1987.

A prolific and respected man of letters throughout his lifetime, Miller died in 2005, aged 89.

CONTEXT

Red Hook

The setting of *A View from the Bridge* is the Red Hook district of Brooklyn, where the longshoremen lived, and it is the immediate neighbourhood of Eddie Carbone, the central character in the play.

From his nearby Brooklyn apartment, Arthur Miller was able to research the lives of the longshoremen and their families. The job of a longshoreman, as we learn from the play, demanded both physical strength and stamina, as well as the ability to withstand the interference and intimidating presence of mafia-style syndicates and unions that aimed to control the workforce and had links to organized crime.

Work was erratic and sometimes a longshoreman would go weeks without being employed. In the play, Eddie explains to Alfieri how he survived the hard times by travelling miles to alternative dockyards to find enough work to feed the family, especially Catherine when she was a child.

Red Hook was originally a Dutch settlement, established in 1636 when the early settlers arrived from Europe. Its name was derived from the red clay soil of the region and the 'hook' shape of its peninsula that projects into the East River estuary. Thousands of dockworkers and their families lived in overcrowded brick tenements there, like the one where Eddie and Beatrice play host to Beatrice's cousins, Marco and Rodolpho. In the early part of the 20th century, it was a tough place to live; legend has it that it was the neighbourhood where the notorious gangster Al Capone started out as a small-time criminal in the 1920s. Around 21,000 people lived in the neighbourhood and the docks were the busiest in the country.

AL CAPONE

Originally from Naples, Al Capone (also known as 'Scarface') was a notorious gangster and mob leader who pursued a life of crime, first in New York and then in Chicago. Characters based on him have appeared in several American gangster movies, such as *Al Capone* (1959), *Scarface* (1983) and *The Untouchables* (1987).

Traditionally a home to various immigrant communities, including the Irish, Germans and Norwegians, by the early 20th century the district had largely become populated with Italian immigrants and their descendants. Indeed, Eddie Carbone refers to the fact that his father came and settled in America. He tells Beatrice, 'I was just thinkin' before, comin' home, suppose my father didn't come to this country, and I was starvin' like them over there... and I had people in America could keep me a couple of months? The man would be honored to lend me a place to sleep.' As the son of a Polish immigrant to America himself, Miller was especially sensitive to the struggles facing those seeking to make a new life in a strange country.

The Brooklyn Bridge

The Brooklyn Bridge, over the East River estuary in New York, was built between 1869 and 1883 and opened in May 1883. It was the first bridge in the world to be suspended by steel and was also the longest suspension bridge in the world at that time, stretching for just over a mile in length, connecting the largely working-class neighbourhood of Brooklyn with the more upmarket Manhattan.

The immediately recognizable rigid steel struts of the bridge have influenced many set designers of *A View from the Bridge*. The now iconic Brooklyn Bridge was originally the only land connection between Manhattan and Brooklyn and remained so for many years, although in modern New York there are now several separate crossings.

Key term

omniscient narrator
a storyteller who knows all there is to know about the story

The Brooklyn Bridge is 'the' bridge of the title of the play and from which Alfieri is supposed to view the action as the **omniscient narrator** who already knows the outcome of Eddie's tragic 'journey'.

It was on this bridge that Miller first saw a piece of graffiti, written in Italian, which read: 'Dove Pete Panto?' ('Where is Pete Panto?'). His curiosity piqued, Miller began to ask around and discovered that Pete Panto was an Italian American who worked on the waterfront. He had stood up to the corrupt union bosses and lost his life in the process.

Immigration from Europe to America

Immigration gathered pace from 1870 to 1914 as European immigrants flooded into the United States in their millions to escape poverty or to seek religious freedoms denied to them in their homelands.

By the 1920s, however, immigrants began to face discrimination, and a cap was imposed by the US government to limit numbers. Immigrants with the correct papers who wanted to settle permanently could still apply for citizenship, provided that they passed rigorous physical and mental health checks on arrival at the Ellis Island Immigration Center in Upper New York Bay. Numbers were restricted and not all applicants were successful.

Workers who wanted to come to work in the United States to earn money to send home, but who planned to return home, like Marco, were not eligible to enter the USA legally. Many resorted to gaining entry illegally, depending upon corrupt middlemen who effectively smuggled them in for a hefty fee. The criminal syndicates that got them into the USA ensured that they had work on the waterfront, for example, at least until they had paid off what they owed. As Eddie tells the brothers Marco and Rodolpho, 'as long as you owe them money, they'll get you plenty of work'.

Codes of honour

The Sicilian immigrants continued to live according to the codes of behaviour and customs of the 'old' country. Unwritten rules about respect and honour within the family and the wider community continued to shape the way they lived their lives. Working hard, protecting the family and family name; showing loyalty to family and pursuing revenge when provoked; these were the values that Eddie Carbone adhered to before the arrival of Rodolpho and Marco.

In *A View from the Bridge,* Miller explores the way in which the codes of behaviour of the older generation were being challenged, particularly through Catherine, who wants to work and make her own way in the world, and Rodolpho. Their mutual love of contemporary popular songs, like 'Paper Doll', and their interest in the movies, shows them to be part of the emerging youth culture in post-war America.

Faced with the imminent loss of Catherine, Eddie's traditional values are strained when he learns from Alfieri that the only recourse that he has to American law is through the betrayal of his Italian code of honour and of Beatrice's cousins, by reporting them to the authorities. Eddie's act of betrayal and its consequences expose Eddie to the wrath of the Sicilian community in Red Hook, as well as to Marco's determination to have his revenge.

Family and home life in Red Hook

In Red Hook, most families lived in crowded tenement buildings with two families on each floor; private bathrooms were unusual, although the Carbone household appears to have one. Family ties were highly important and if relatives arrived, legally or otherwise, in the immigrant areas of New York, it would have been considered dishonourable not to find a space for them in the family home.

TENEMENT HOUSES

Tenement houses existed in most inner-city areas across the Western world in the early part of the 20th century. They are large houses that have been divided up for multiple occupancy, often by landlords with limited concern for the safety and comfort of their tenants.

The older immigrant population tended to cling on to the traditions of their country of origin; marriages still had to be approved by the families and it was traditional for a young man to ask the father for his daughter's hand in marriage.

Older women rarely worked outside the home. As Eddie says to Beatrice, when she questions his views about the job that Catherine wants to take, 'You lived in a house all your life, what do you know about it? You never worked in your life.'

However, by the 1950s, things began to change. Second- and third-generation Italian-Americans were losing touch with some of the customs of their parents and grandparents. Younger immigrants wanted more freedom and embraced the emerging American culture of the 1950s, including the 'American Dream' (see below). Few women continued to work after getting married, but single women were beginning to look for respectable jobs outside the domestic sphere. Eddie clearly has ambitions for Catherine and has supported her, first through high school and then through secretarial school. Catherine is delighted to be offered the job of stenographer (someone who transcribes speech in shorthand) in a large plumbing company, but Eddie wants better for her, 'I want you to be in a nice office. Maybe a lawyer's office someplace in New York.'

The American Dream

The concept of the 'American Dream' appeared first in James Truslow Adams' book *The Epic of America* (1931). It was based upon an idea taken from the American Declaration of Independence from Great Britain that all men are created equal with the right to life, liberty and the pursuit of happiness. America was seen as a land of opportunity, particularly for immigrant workers like Marco and Rodolpho who were prepared to work hard to achieve prosperity.

The theatrical context of the play

In the 1930s and 1940s, four highly talented new American playwrights challenged established dramatic conventions of the American stage with their serious yet popular plays.

Eugene O'Neill (1888–1953) is credited with transforming American theatre from a form dominated by melodrama to one devoted to revealing the 'inner lives' of the characters. Influenced by theatrical innovations in Europe, O'Neill's plays include *The Hairy Ape* (1922), *Mourning becomes Electra* (1931), *The Iceman Cometh* (1939) and the epic *Long Day's Journey into Night* (1941), all of which contributed to his international reputation as a theatrical innovator.

Our Town (1938) by Thornton Wilder (1897–1975) opens on a stage with 'No Curtain. No Scenery' and with the 'Stage Manager' directly addressing the audience, introducing them to 'Grover's Corners', a fictional town representing 'every' town in America. The 'Stage Manager' functions like a Greek chorus, assuming control over the action, 'prompting' actors and 'cueing' scene changes; possibly anticipating Miller's use of Alfieri in *A View from the Bridge*.

Both Wilder's and O'Neill's work inspired Tennessee Williams (1911–1983) and Arthur Miller to experiment with dramatic form.

Williams first won critical acclaim in 1944 with *The Glass Menagerie*, a 'memory play' partly narrated by the main character, Tom, looking back over his teenage years. In 1947, both Williams' play *A Streetcar Named Desire* and Miller's *All My Sons* had highly successful debuts.

Miller wrote in his autobiography, *Timebends*, how Williams' *Streetcar* had changed the way that he was thinking about his playwriting. '*Streetcar*' he wrote, 'opened one specific door for me. Not the story or the characters or the direction, but the words and their liberation, the joy of the writer in writing them, the radiant eloquence of its composition, moved me more than all its pathos' (page 182).

box set
a set mainly used in naturalistic drama that is created to look like a real room, with windows and doors and furnishings appropriate to the period setting. The audience views the action through an invisible 'fourth wall' that completes the 'box'

composite set
a set that accommodates two or more different settings or locations on stage; composite sets are used for plays that do not demand a fully naturalistic style

soliloquy
a speech spoken by a character, directly to the audience, or as if to themselves

In both *Death of a Salesman* (1949) and *A View from the Bridge*, Miller experiments with the dramatic possibilities of manipulating both time and space on stage. In *Death of a Salesman*, the protagonist, Willy Loman, exists both in the present and in the past, in his memories and imagination. The stage space is used fluidly, with Miller replacing the traditional naturalistic **box set** by a **composite set**, with characters entering and exiting, on occasion, through 'walls' and across time.

In *A View from the Bridge*, Alfieri recalls a story from the past, which is played out for the audience in the present. The narrative is interrupted by Alfieri's flashbacks to past interviews that he has had with Eddie or with Marco and Rodolpho. Miller adapts the stage convention of the **soliloquy**, whereby Alfieri addresses the audience directly, in the present, but is not noticed by the other characters on stage, who continue with their past lives, oblivious to his presence.

Miller also employed a composite set, whereby the audience can see both the interior of the Carbone apartment and the street outside the tenement block. Alfieri's office, the reception room of the jail and a telephone booth are also present as part of the same setting. Designers frequently also suggest that the action takes place in the shadow of the Brooklyn Bridge on stage. Miller's intention that the bridge 'view' represents that of middle-class Americans, travelling over the bridge and looking down on the tragic events unfolding in Red Hook.

A View from the Bridge has been in continuous production in one part of the world or another since its first successful London debut in 1956. A recent revival by Belgian director Ivo van Hove caused a sensation, both at the Young Vic in London (2014) and on its transfer to Broadway (2015), because of its 'stripped back' treatment.

Instead of the composite set as described above, designer Jan Versweyveld offered a bare stage, edged with a narrow black glass 'sill' for actors to sit on or lean against. No props were used; there was no furniture of any kind, only the chair for Marco to lift, weapon-like, above Eddie's head, which appeared when it was needed. The cast were barefoot, and the costumes were free from any real indications of period.

Emulating Miller's original intentions when he wrote his one-act version, van Hove dispensed with the interval and ratcheted-up the tension in one complete 'arc', as Miller has often described the unfolding of the play's plot.

Genre

In *A View from the Bridge,* Miller applies a blend of dramatic forms, including tragedy and social realism, to create a hybrid form with a wide audience appeal.

Though Miller abandoned his first version of the play, which echoed classical Greek tragedy both in its use of verse and in its single 'Act' of continuous action, *A View from the Bridge* has many similarities to Greek tragic drama.

The features of Greek tragedy

All classical Greek tragedies follow the same model and involve the fall of a great man (the **tragic hero**) from greatness to misery because of a character flaw (weakness). His journey or 'tragic arc' also involves setbacks and reversals of fortune that build to a climax and end in **catastrophe** for him. The tragic hero experiences a **tragic recognition** of his own contribution to his ruin.

In Greek tragedy, the fall of the hero affects the wider society or state in which he had previously been powerful and/or respected. The audience are expected to undergo a '**cathartic** experience' of pity for the defeated **protagonist** and fear, lest a similarly tragic ending ruins their lives. Another important element of Greek tragedy is the role of the chorus. The chorus figures were frequently representative of wise Greek citizens or 'elders', who comment on the action as it unfolds; they also participate in the action through their interaction with key characters. In *A View from the Bridge*, the role of the chorus is taken by Alfieri, whose voice and 'view' guides the audience through Eddie's tragic experience.

Miller deviates from the classical model in two key areas: first, he adopts an ordinary man as the protagonist of the play rather than the great leader of men typical in Greek times, and second, he not only abandons the highly poetic language of the Greek playwrights but actually writes in the colloquial language of those native to Brooklyn. In an article written in the late 1940s, Miller stated his belief that 'the common man is as apt a subject for tragedy... as kings were', describing the 'tragic hero' as simply an 'individual attempting to gain his rightful position in his society' (*The Theatre Essays of Arthur Miller*, 1978).

Key terms

catastrophe
in Greek tragedy, the concluding part of the play where the protagonist accepts ruin

catharsis
the intended audience experience at the end of the tragedy, purging them of the emotions of pity and fear

protagonist
the main character

tragic hero
the main character who falls from greatness to misery because of a character flaw

tragic recognition
(*anagnorisis*) recognition that the tragedy has been self-inflicted

Realism

Realism is a style of theatre that depends upon an appearance of real life being presented on the stage. The audience looks into 'a room' or sees locations that look similar to those in real life. Realistic action takes place chronologically and characters interact using dialogue that mirrors natural speech. The play proceeds logically from the initial situation presented, through a series of developments or complications, to the final denouement where the plot comes to a fitting conclusion, either resolving issues satisfactorily for the main character(s) or concluding unhappily.

Social realism is a genre adopted by writers and artists who use a realistic approach and focus their work on everyday life, usually on the working classes, the poor or the destitute; the work generally involves criticism of dominant social structures. *A View from the Bridge* is located in a poor part of New York, where families lead a hand-to-mouth existence. Eddie's story has an uncle's incestuous desire for his niece at its centre, and a question mark hangs both over Rodolpho's sexuality and over his motives in marrying Catherine. In line with the expectations of social realism, Miller questions the personal morality of both Eddie and Rodolpho as well as the public morality of the American authorities' attitudes towards illegal immigrants who have come to the USA to escape starvation and/or persecution in their home country.

A View from the Bridge in the 21st Century

Though written over 60 years ago, *A View from the Bridge* has never appeared dated because it explores universal themes, such as community and loyalty, love, passion and personal identity. It also foregrounds the controversial topic of immigration, which is as relevant today as it has ever been.

Ivo van Hove's sensational revival in 2014 brought the play to huge new audiences on both sides of the Atlantic, homing in, as it did, on Miller's searing exploration of sexual taboos as well as on the raw human emotions underpinning all family conflict.

The bridge of the title also implies the metaphorical bridge between different peoples: between American citizens and foreign immigrants and the metaphorical bridge between different stages of life, for Catherine for example, between girlhood and womanhood.

ACTIVITIES

Plot

1 In Alfieri's first speech to the audience, he warns them that the play will end badly, as it runs 'its bloody course'. What effects does Miller achieve by alerting the audience to the inevitable unhappy ending of the plot?

Think about:

- how the audience experience is affected by the knowledge
- how they will relate to Alfieri as an omniscient narrator figure.

2 What are your first impressions of the relationships between members of the Carbone family at the beginning of Act One?

Jot down your thoughts, supported by relevant quotations, and consider:

- Eddie's attitude towards Catherine, her new clothes and her desire to start work
- the relationship between Eddie and Beatrice
- Catherine's feelings towards her aunt and uncle.

Key term

family dynamic
the various relationships within the family unit

3 How does the arrival of the cousins change the **family dynamic** in Act One of the play? Make notes about the different reactions of Beatrice, Catherine and Eddie to the new guests. How might these reactions be highlighted in a performance?

Remember to look at the stage directions as well as the dialogue, noting down relevant quotations.

4 What impact does Miller create by ending Act One as he does?

Re-read the final sequence of the action, from Catherine's line on page 53:

> **Catherine** *[Flushed with revolt]* You wanna dance, Rodolpho?
>
> **Eddie** *freezes.*

Make a note of how Miller builds tension to the end of the Act. Look closely at the stage directions as well as the dialogue.

Key terms

falling action
events after
the climax. In
*A View from
the Bridge*, the
climax may be
identified as
Eddie's call to
the Immigration
Bureau

rising action
the events in a
play that lead
up to its climax

5   How does the structure of the play, in two acts only and with 'interventions' from Alfieri, help to intensify the building tension that leads to the bloody finale?

a)   First, track the moments that contribute to the rising tension in the play; make a note of relevant quotations.

b)   Plan your essay for this question, including key quotations. You may like to include:

- Alfieri's role as a 'chorus' figure, developing a relationship with the audience
- his ability to 'compress' time, so that events that are actually months apart seem to occur in rapid succession
- the **rising action** of anticipation; the **falling action** of regret.

c)   Write your essay.

Context

6   Watch the 1954 film *On the Waterfront*, starring Marlon Brando and directed by Elia Kazan. This film offers an authentic insight into the living and working conditions of the dockworkers and their families, and could inform your setting and costume ideas for Miller's play.

7   In the play, Eddie tells Beatrice not to worry about getting the apartment ready for her cousins, saying, 'Listen, they'll think it's a millionaire's house compared to the way they live'. Go back through the play and note down what the cousins say about the living and working conditions in Sicily.

What dramatic effects do you think Miller achieved through comparing and contrasting post-war America and Italy?

8 Consider how far Eddie's betrayal of his wife's family can be justified, or at least understood.

Focus on the following quotations and use them to support your discussion (verbal or written).

a) The Vinny Bolzano story:

> 'The whole neighborhood was cryin'.'
>
> 'You'll never see him no more, a guy do a thing like that? How's he gonna show his face?'

b) Alfieri's advice to Eddie:

> 'You won't have a friend in the world, Eddie! Even those who understand will turn against you, even the ones who feel the same will despise you!'

c) Catherine's condemnation of Eddie:

> 'He bites people when they sleep! He comes when nobody's lookin' and poisons decent people. In the garbage he belongs!'

Character

9 To what extent can Eddie Carbone be seen as a hero?

Identify moments from the play where Eddie:

- is considered to be a 'hero' by others
- falls from 'greatness' (identify his 'tragic flaw' and what causes his 'fall')
- recognizes his self-inflicted tragedy
- accepts ruin/catastrophe

or simply:

- struggles 'to gain his 'rightful' position in his society'.

10 **a)** How do Catherine's feelings change towards Eddie in the course of the play? Use quotations from the text to support your ideas.

And/or:

b) How would you perform the role of Catherine in three or four key moments from the play, to reveal her changing feelings to the audience?

You might consider Catherine's:

- use of voice; delivery of key lines

- reactions to what Eddie says to her

- use of space; closeness to or distance from Eddie on stage; eye contact; non-verbal communication; facial expressions, gesture and movement.

11 Compare and contrast the characters of Marco and Rodolpho using evidence from the text. What dramatic effects does Miller create through his presentation of the two brothers?

12 What do you think the characters of Louis and Mike contribute to the drama? Consider their roles as representative of the Red Hook 'community'.

13 What effects are achieved by including Alfieri as a character within the play as well as being the narrator of Eddie's fateful story? Use the text to support your ideas.

14 Does the presentation of Beatrice's character traits make her appear to be a good wife to Eddie? Does she appear to be a good role model to Catherine? Support your ideas with quotations from the text.

Language

Miller includes a variety of language to reflect the backgrounds of individual characters.

- Alfieri: speaks using the formal language of an educated lawyer

- Eddie, Beatrice, Catherine, Louis, Mike: speak in Brooklynese, the dialect of the neighbourhood; their speech includes features of colloquial expression

- Marco and Rodolpho: both speak using a non-standard American idiom; Marco says little and uses halting phrases; Rodolpho is more expansive and fluent in English.

15 **a)** Look back through the play and find examples that exemplify these different styles of language.

b) Analyse Miller's use of language in the section starting on page 22, when the cousins first arrive. Explain the effects that Miller creates here. The section begins 'He was as good a man as he had to be in a life that was hard and even' and ends on page 26 with '[smiling] He trusts his wife'.

16 Some words are repeated several times and used by different characters and in different contexts throughout the play. Repeated words include: love, family, respect, name, baby.

Find these words in the text and make brief comments about their significance *and* the significance of their repeated use.

17 In Act One, Eddie describes Catherine as looking like a madonna; later in the act he asks her 'What's the high heels for, Garbo?'

Explain the effects created by Miller's inclusion of these two different stereotypes of womanhood in reference to Catherine.

18 Look up the full lyrics of the song 'Paper Doll' by Johnny Black on the Internet. Explain why you think Miller chose this particular song for Rodolpho to sing in Act One and how it relates to the action of the play.

Themes

19 How would you perform the role of Alfieri in three or four different sections of the play in order to highlight for your audience his role as a 'champion' of the law?

Consider Alfieri's physical presence on stage – his vocal qualities and delivery of lines. Look at his direct address to the audience as well as his interactions with Eddie or with Marco and Rodolpho.

20 Discuss the idea that love is the most important theme in *A View from the Bridge*.

You should consider Miller's presentation of different forms of love in the play, for example, romantic, familial and sexual.

THE PRESENTATION OF LOVE

Familial love (love for family members) includes maternal love (such as what Beatrice feels for Catherine, even though she is a 'surrogate' mother to her), avuncular love (non-sexual love of an uncle for his nieces and/or nephews) and fraternal love (love between brothers).

Sexual love relationships include incestuous love (where one family member feels inappropriately sexual feelings towards a relative), homosexual love (where love exists between two members of the same gender) and heterosexual love (where love exists between members of the opposite gender).

21 Repeat the previous activity ('Discuss the idea that... is the most important theme in *A View from the Bridge*') substituting the following themes:

- justice
- respect
- self-realization
- loyalty.

Remember to suggest alternative themes if you consider them to be more important.

22 Reread the final section of the play, starting from page 82 with 'What do you want! Eddie, what do you want!' and continuing to the end of the play.

Either:

a) Explain how Miller builds tension as the 'bloody course' of the play reaches its inevitable conclusion.

Or:

b) Direct other members in your group to create a thrilling final spectacle for your audience.

Consider the group dynamic on stage: the use of a crowd of 'extras', the use of space, as well as the usual dramatic methods of employing the actors' appearances, and their vocal, physical and facial expressions to achieve your aims.

Performance and genre

 Do some internet research into early and more contemporary productions of the play; in particular, look for contrasting naturalistic and non-naturalistic approaches to interpreting the drama.

Now, outline your ideas for set and/or costume designs for the play; give full reasons for your choices.

NATURALISTIC AND NON-NATURALISTIC STAGING

Naturalistic staging attempts to imitate settings and costumes that we might expect to see in real life, for example with apparently 'real' doors, windows, furnishings on stage for interior settings or with apparently 'real' trees, grass, flowers, streams on stage for exterior settings; costumes are appropriate for the action and relate to a distinct time period.

Non-naturalistic staging makes no such attempt to replicate reality but provides a useable space for the action to take place in and may include abstract design elements; costumes may be symbolic or represent a range of different periods across the cast, to suggest that what the play is communicating is universally relevant.

24 Choose any two-page spread of text that includes key moments of action or dialogue. In groups, read sections of the text aloud, always having someone to read the stage directions aloud. Make a note of those stage directions that convey additional meaning or subtext to the lines, helping the potential audience to understand the thought behind the words.

Either:

a) Explain what each stage direction on your chosen pages will convey to an audience.

Or:

b) Act out the section, remembering to follow the stage directions precisely as written; evaluate the impact of acting out the stage directions.

25 Look closely at each of Alfieri's appearances in the play and consider the following:

a) Would you describe Alfieri as an impartial chorus figure, offering only objective facts, or is he more subjective in his presentation of Eddie's story?

Look for quotations that support your opinion.

b) If you were performing the role of Alfieri, explain how you would distinguish between the character fulfilling his 'choric' role and the character interacting with Eddie and the other characters.